Yogasanas & Pranayama

Swami Ramesh Chandra Shukla

Published by:

V&S PUBLISHERS

F-2/16, Ansari Road, Daryaganj, New Delhi-110002
☎ 011-23240026, 011-23240027 • *Fax:* 011-23240028
Email: info@vspublishers.com • *Website:* www.vspublishers.com

Regional Office : Hyderabad
5-1-707/1, Brij Bhawan (Beside Central Bank of India Lane)
Bank Street, Koti, Hyderabad - 500 095
☎ 040-24737290
E-mail: vspublishershyd@gmail.com

Branch Office : Mumbai
Jaywant Industrial Estate, 2nd Floor-222, Tardeo Road
Opposite Sobo Central, Mumbai - 400 034
☎ 022-23510736
E-mail: vspublishersmum@gmail.com

Follow us on:   

All books available at **www.vspublishers.com**

ISBN 978-93-505705-9-3
Edition 2016

Printed at : Param Offseters, Okhla, New Delhi-110020

Publisher's Note

After a number of bestsellers on Health, V&S Publishers have now come up with this unique and exclusive book on Yoga called ***Yogasanas & Pranayama***. The book has been authored by **Swami Ramesh Chandra Shukla**, an *exponent and veteran in this field.* Many renowned scholars and Yoga experts like Swami Chetananand, Vishwajyoti (Yoga teacher in Rajasthan), Shri Amit Kumar (Yoga Teacher), Dr. S. K. Pandey (Yoga Consultant), Dr. Vishad Tripathi (Vedic Scientist), Dr. Virendra Parivrajak (Yoga Teacher), etc have also given their valuable suggestions and inputs during the compilation of the book.

The true essence of Yoga revolves around elevating the life force or 'Kundalini' at the base of the spine. Basically, it aims to achieve this through a series of physical and mental exercises. At the physical level, the methods consist of various *yoga postures or asanas* that aim to keep the body healthy. The mental techniques include breathing exercises or *pranayama* and meditation or *dhyana* to discipline the mind. Therefore, Yoga is not merely a fitness regime or a religion; it is a way of living whose aim is 'a healthy mind in a healthy body'.

The main aim in publishing such books is to create a *health and fitness regime among our esteemed readers, who have definitely become very health conscious in the present world.* Moreover, Yoga does not just offer a natural and permanent remedy to the various types of physical ailments that human beings suffer from, it also nourishes and enlightens our brain and the Soul.

The author in this book has explained thoroughly *the concept of Yoga, the significance of Yoga in the contemporary world, Surya-Namaskar* (Sun Salutation), the various types of *Asanas* to cure different types of diseases, some of them being as fatal as *Cancer, AIDS, severe male and female Genital Problems, Diabetes, Kidney Problems,* etc.

Hence Readers, the book is beneficial to all and a Must Read for both the young and the old, irrespective of age, sex or social status in the society. Hope you enjoy reading as well as practising some of the Asanas that you feel are suitable for you with of course, the advice and guidance of a doctor to help you stay fit, disease-free, happy and healthy.

Contents

Preface

The present book is the result of my curious search for the quest of absolute truth and that too in true relevance to the day to day life of people to fight back with the stress and the ill-health caused due to that stress.

After my retirement from the Government service, I was highly inclined towards the *samskaras* which I inherited from my parents and grandparents during my childhood days to college life. These *samskaras* are the only base for self-realisation and ultimate freedom in our lives, which decides our spiritual destiny. I indulged myself into the core of spiritual activities under the supervision of the renowned spiritual masters.

After few years, I realised the rise of my consciousness and the practical aspects of the philosophy of the Yoga began to rise through my consciousness. Then I started teaching these spiritual activities. This spiritual activity gave me that internal spiritual strength which became the cause of the spiritual as well as mental and physical growth of people at many places.

In this book, I have utilised all my knowledge which I gained through my experiences throughout. Such knowledge will be surely helpful for those people who are helpless in curing their day to day problems of mental, physical and spiritual health and didn't find the solution to these problems even after trying so many methods to cure them.

I have tried my level best to explain the most complex fundamentals of Yoga in a very easy terminology and methodology so as to make even a layman understand this divine philosophy for the best of its use in his life for his mental, physical and spiritual growth.

I would also like to thank those scholars and experts such as, Swami Chetananand, Vishwajyoti (yoga teacher in Rajasthan), Shri Amit Kumar (Yoga Teacher), Dr. S. K. Pandey (Yoga Consultant), Dr. Vishad Tripathi (Vedic Scientist), Dr. Virendra Parivrajak (Yoga Teacher), Rajesh Gupta

(Yoga Teacher), Savita Mishra (Yoga Teacher) – who helped me during the compilation of this book.

Lastly, I would wish all my readers who would read this book, a heartily successful, blissful and healthy life in all the spheres of Mind, Body and Soul.

Chapter 1

What is Yoga?

The word, **Yoga** comes from the Sanskrit word, '**Yuj**, meaning to *yoke, join* or *unite*. It implies joining or integrating all aspects of the individual-body with mind, and mind with soul to achieve a balanced and healthy lifestyle so that we can spiritually unite with the Supreme. *According to the Yoga Sutras of Patanjali*, the ultimate aim of Yoga is to reach '**Kaivalya**' *(emanicipation or ultimate freedom)*.

Yoga is commonly known as a generic term for physical, mental and spiritual discipline originating from ancient India and found in *Sanatana Dharma (Hinduism)*. It envisioned in one of the six spiritual schools of Vedic (Hindu) philosophy known as the '**Shat-Darshana**'. The Yoga school of philosophy accepts the *Sankhya school of philosophy* and its metaphysics as both these schools belong to the class of the *Shat-Darshana.* Yoga is not a matter of psychology of mental health only but it is a question of spiritual growth. Yoga practices are an attempt to push the individual towards his true potential as a complete *self-realisation.* The whole system of Yoga is built on three main structures – *exercise, breathing* and *meditation* thereby leading towards full psyche control of the SELF in order to achieve the ultimate freedom as discussed above.

These six schools of philosophy are:

1. Samkhya
2. Yoga
3. Nyaya
4. Vaisheshika
5. Purva (Karma) Mimamsa
6. Uttar Mimamsa (Vedanta): The Three Schools of Vedanta
    (a) Monism: Advaita Vedanta
    (b) Qualified Monism: Vishistadvaita
    (c) Dualism: Dvaita
    (d) Synthesis: Achintya Bheda-Abheda Vedanta

1. Samkhya

Samkhya is widely regarded to be the oldest of the philosophical systems of the Vedic tradition. Its philosophy regards the universe as consisting of two eternal realities: *purusha* and *prakrti*. The purushas (souls) are many, conscious and devoid of all qualities. They are the silent spectators of prakrti (matter or nature), which is composed of three *gunas* (dispositions): *satva*, *rajas* and *tamas* (steadiness, activity and dullness). When the equilibrium of the *gunas* is disturbed, the world order evolves. This disturbance is due to the proximity of Purusha and Prakrti. Liberation (*kaivalya*), then, consists of the realisation of the difference between the two. This was a dualistic philosophy. But there are differences between the Samkhya and Western forms of dualism. In the West, the fundamental distinction is between mind and body. In *Samkhya*, however, it is between the self (purusha) and matter, and the latter incorporates what Westerners would normally refer to as 'mind'.

2. Yoga

The *Yoga* system is generally considered to have arisen from the *Samkhya philosophy*. Its primary text is the ***Bhagavad Gita***, which explores the four primary systems. Sage ***Patanjali*** wrote an extremely influential text on *Raja Yoga* (or meditation) entitled the *Yoga Sutra*. The most significant difference from *Samkhya* is that the *Yoga school* not only incorporates the concept of ***Ishvara*** (a personal God) into its metaphysical worldview, which the *Samkhya* does not, but also upholds Ishvara as the ideal upon which to meditate. This is because *Ishvara is the only aspect* of purusha that has not become entangled with prakrti. It also utilises the ***Brahman/Atman*** terminology and concepts that are found in depth in the Upanishads, thus breaking from the *Samkhya* school by adopting *Vedantic monist* concepts. The Yoga system lays down elaborate prescriptions for gradually gaining physical and mental control and mastery over the personal, aspects the body and mind, self, until one's consciousness has intensified sufficiently to allow awareness of one's real Self (the soul, or Atman) (as distinct from one's feelings, thoughts and actions). Realisation of the goal of Yoga is known as ***moksha***, ***nirvana*** and ***Samadhi***. They all speak to the realisation of the *Atman* as being nothing other than the infinite Brahman.

3. Nyaya

The *Nyaya* School of philosophical speculation is based on a text called the *Nyaya Sutra*. It was written by ***Gautama*** (not to be confused with the

founder of Buddhism), also known as ***Akshapada***. The most important contribution made by this school is its methodology. This is based on a system of logic that has subsequently been adopted by most of the other Vedic schools much in the same way that Western science, religion and philosophy and can be said to be largely based on *Aristotelian logic*. But Nyaya is not merely logic for its own sake. The Vedic seers believed that obtaining valid knowledge was the only way to obtain release from suffering. They therefore took great pains to identify valid sources of knowledge and to distinguish these from mere false opinions. According to the Nyaya School, there are exactly four sources of knowledge (***pramanas***): *perception, inference, comparison* and *testimony*. Knowledge obtained through each of these can of course still be either valid or invalid, and the Nyaya scholars again went to great pains to identify, in each case, what it took to make knowledge valid, in the process coming up with a number of *explanatory schemes*. In this sense, *Nyaya* is probably the closest *Vedic* equivalent to contemporary *Western analytical philosophy*. An important later development in *Nyaya* is the system of *Navya Nyaya* (New Logic).

4. Vaisheshika

The *Vaisheshika* system, which was founded by the sage ***Kanada***, postulates an atomic pluralism. In terms of this school of thought, all objects in the physical universe are reducible to a certain number of atoms. Although the Vaishesika system developed independently from the Nyaya, the two eventually merged because of their closely related metaphysical theories. In its classical form, however, the Vaishesika School differed from the Nyaya in one crucial respect: where Nyaya accepted four sources of valid knowledge, the Vaishesika accepted only perception and inference.

5. Purva (karma) Mimamsa

The main objective of the *Purva* ("earlier") *Mimamsa School* was to establish the authority of the Vedas. Consequently, this school's most valuable contribution to Hinduism was its formulation of the rules of Vedic interpretation. Its adherents believed that revelation must be proved by reasoning, that it should not be accepted blindly as dogma. In keeping with this belief, they laid great emphasis on *dharma*, which they understood as the performance of Vedic rituals. The *Mimamsa* accepted the logical and philosophical teachings of the other schools, but felt that these paid insufficient attention to the right actions. They believed that the other schools of thought, who pursued *moksha* (salvation) as their ultimate aim, were not completely free from desire and selfishness. In Vedic tradition, we are all illuminated under the light of God. When we have *moksha*, we believe that

we become closer to God. According to the *Mimamsa*, the very striving for liberation stemmed from a selfish desire to be free. Only by acting in accordance with the prescriptions of the Vedas could one attain salvation (rather than liberation). At a later stage, however, the Mimamsa School changed its views in this regard and began to teach the doctrines of God and ***mukti*** (freedom). Its adherents then advocated the release or escape from the soul from its constraints through what was known as *gyaan* (enlightened activity). While *Mimamsa* does not receive much scholarly attention these days, its influence can be felt in the life of the practising present day Hindus. All Hindu rituals, ceremonies and religious laws are influenced by it.

6. Uttar Mimamsa (Vedanta): The Three Schools of Vedanta

The *Uttar* ('later') *Mimamsa* School, more commonly known as the ***Vedanta***, concentrates on the philosophical teachings of the ***Upanishads*** rather than on the ritualistic injunctions of the ***Brahmans***. While the traditional Vedic ***'karma kanda'*** (ritualistic components of religion) continued to be practised as meditative and propitiatory rites gearing society (through the Brahmins) to self-knowledge, more *gyaan* (knowledge) centered understandings began to emerge, mystical streams of Vedic religion that focussed on meditation, self-discipline and spiritual connectivity rather than more practical aspects of religion like rituals and rites. The more abstruse *Vedanta* (meaning literally the end of the Vedas) is the essence of the Vedas, encapsulated in the Upanishads which are commentaries on the four original books (***Rig***, ***Yajur***, ***Sama*** and ***Atharva***). The Vedantic thought drew on the Vedic cosmology, hymns and philosophy. The *first Upanishad*, the ***Brihadaranyaka***, appeared thousands of years ago. While thirteen or so Upanishads are accepted as principal, over one hundred exist. The most influential Vedantic thought, based on the Upanishads, considers the consciousness of the **Self** – ***Jivatma*** – to be continuous with and indistinguishable from the consciousness of the **Supreme or Brahman** –***Paramatma***. Their systematization into one coherent treatise was undertaken by ***Badarayanacharya (Veda Vyasa)***, in a work called the *Vedanta Sutra*, and also known as *Brahma-Sutra.* The cryptic way in which the aphorisms of the *Vedanta sutras* are presented leaves the door wide open for a multitude of interpretations. This led to a proliferation of Vedanta schools. Each of these interprets the texts in its own way and has produced its own series of sub-commentaries – all claiming to be faithful to the original.

(a) Monism: Advaita Vedanta

Advaita Vedanta is probably the *best known of all Vedanta schools*. Advaita literally means "not two"; thus this is what we refer to as a monistic (or non-dualistic) system, which emphasizes oneness. Its first great consolidator was ***Shankaracharya***. Continuing the line of thought of some of the Upanishad teachers, and also that of his own teacher *Gaudapada*, *Shankara* expounded the doctrine of Advaita – a nondualistic reality. By analyzing the three states of experience (waking, dreaming and deep sleep) each of these related with a nature and level of speech *(vak)* as described in earlier chapters, he exposed the relative nature of the world and established the supreme truth of the Advaita: the nondual reality of ***Brahman*** in which *atman* (the individual soul) and *Brahman* (the ultimate reality expressed in the ***trimurti***) are identified absolutely. However, many more see ***Adi Shankaracharya*** drawing from the monist concepts that were visibly ingrained in formerly existing texts, like the more abstruse sections of the Vedas as well as the older Upanishads. Subsequent Vedantins debated whether the reality of Brahman was ***saguna*** (with attributes) or ***nirguna*** (without attributes). Belief in the concept of ***Saguna Brahman*** gave rise to a proliferation of devotional attitudes and more widespread worship of Vishnu and Shiva. Advaita Vedanta is strictly grounded in a belief that the ultimate truth is ***Nirguna Brahman***. The *Vishistadvaita* and *Dvaita* schools believed in an ultimately saguna Brahman.

(b) Qualified Monism: Vishistadvaita

Ramanujaacharya was the foremost proponent of the concept of ***Sriman Narayana*** as the supreme Brahman. He taught that Ultimate reality had three aspects: ***Ishvara*** (***Vishnu***), ***chetant*** (soul) and ***avchetant*** (matter). Vishnu is the only independent reality, while souls and matter are dependent on God for their existence. Because of this qualification of Ultimate reality, Ramanuja's system is known as qualified non-dualism.

(c) Dualism: Dvaita

Like ***Ramanujaachrya***, ***Madhvaacharya*** identified God with Vishnu, but his view of reality was purely dualistic and is therefore called ***Dvaita*** (dualistic).

(d) Synthesis

Ahintya Bheda-Abheda Vedanta Chaitanya Mahaprabhu, a devotee of ***Krishna (Vishnu)***, proposed a synthesis between the monist and dualist philosophies by stating that the soul is equally distinct (***bheda***) and non-distinct (***abheda***) from God, whom he identified as ***Krishna (Vishnu)***, and that this, although unthinkable (***ahintya***), is experiencable in devotion.

Patanjali is widely regarded as the complier of the *formal Yoga philosophy*. His yoga is known as the **Ashtanga-Yoga** which is a system for the eight-fold control of the body and mind. He defines the word yoga in his second sutra – *yogas chitta-vritti-nirodah* – yoga sutra 1-2, which means "through the Yoga, one must cleanse his *chitta* (mind stuff) impurities thereby achieving complete blissful health".

His **Ashtanga Yoga** has eight limbs. The eight limbs are:

1. **Yama** (The five absentions): Ahimsa (non violence), Satya (truth, non-lying), Astey (non-covetous, Brahmacharya [celibacy] and Aparigraha (non-possessiveness).
2. **Niyama** (The five observances): Sauch (purity), Santosh (contentment), Tapas (austerity), Swadhyaya (study of scriptures) and Ishwar-pranidhana (surrender to God).
3. **Asana**
4. **Pranayama**
5. **Pratyahar** (Abstraction-withdrawal of the sense organs from external objects.
6. **Dharna** (Concentration)
7. **Dhyana** (Meditation)
8. **Samadhi** (Liberation) merging consciousness with the object of meditation.

Thus, we can say that the **Ashtanga-Yoga** can be very useful to practice. You can learn it as **Jnan Yoga** or the yoga of mind, the **Karma Yoga** as yoga of right action and **Bhakti Yoga** as yoga of devotion.

Before practising Yoga, we should eliminate some misconceptions. First is that Yoga is not a *religion.* The other misconception about yoga is that it is an exercise, a way to keep fit. It is not limited in its objective only to look at our physical dimensions but also other deeper dimensions of our life. We should remember that the steady control of our senses and cessation of our mental activity may lead us to our supreme state.

The Bhagavad Gita (song of the Lord) also refers to Yoga in a variety of ways. An entire chapter 6 is dedicated to the traditional yoga practice including meditation. It introduces four prominent types of Yoga – Karma Yoga (the Yoga of Action), Bhakti Yoga (the Yoga of Devotion) and Jnan Yoga (the Yoga of Knowledge) and finally, the *Raja Yoga* which is the

King of the Yogas as it merges the consciousness of the individual SELF into the universal SELF.

Purpose of Yoga

Nature of the *Jiva* (the Soul) and the Means to *Moksha* (Ultimate Liberation): (Nature of the individual soul and the means to Final Liberation):- To Shri Adi Shankaracharya, the *Jiva* or the individual soul is only relatively real. Its individuality lasts only so long as it is subject to unreal *Upadhis* (limiting conditions) due to *Avidya* (ignorance). The *Jiva* identifies itself with the body, mind and the senses, when it is deluded by *Avidya* or ignorance. It thinks, it acts and enjoys, on account of Avidya. In reality, it is not different from the *Brahma* or the Absolute (the universal SELF). The *Upanishads* declare emphatically: *"Tat Tvam Asi" (That Thou Art)*. Just as the bubble (foam) becomes one with the ocean when it bursts, just as the space within a pot becomes one with the universal space when the pot is broken, so also the *Jiva* or the empirical SELF becomes one with *Brahma*, when it gets knowledge of the *Brahma*, that is the self-realisation through Yoga. When knowledge dawns in it through annihilation of Avidya, it is freed from its individuality and finitude and realises its essential *Sat-Chit-Ananda (Existence, Consciousness, and Bliss)* nature. It merges itself in the *ocean of bliss. The river of life joins the ocean of existence*. This is the real and the ultimate Truth. The release from samsara means, according to Yoga philosophy, the absolute merging of the individual soul in Brahma due to dismissal of the erroneous notion that the soul is distinct from Brahma. According to Yoga, *Karma* (actions) and *Bhakti* (devotion) are means to *Jnan* (knowledge) which is *Moksha* (liberation).

Hence, if we take an overall gaze of the philosophy of Yoga, can conclude that Yoga is the only source for all the remedies of the disorders in our lives which pertain to the planes of spiritual, astral, mental and physical. Yoga not only purifies our physical state of bodies but also purifies our heart, mind and soul to such an extent that we can remove and get rid of all the impurities once for the lifetime.

Chapter 2

Relevance of Yoga in the Modern World

In modern times, Yoga is a basic requirement to keep your mind and body healthy. By practising Yoga, you can save a lot of money you spend on your health and ailments.

However, there are certain notions and inhibitions about Yoga in modern times also and these preconceived notions have discouraged many people from practising Yoga.

These mental and moral inhibitions are as under:

- Businessmen and busy men both regard yoga as a wastage of time.
- Luxury living people also avoid yoga.
- Healthy persons believe that they don't need to practise yoga.
- Mostly people think yoga as an exercise to keep their body fit and they ignore the other limbs of yoga.

All these issues and abductions arise from sheer ignorance. We should remember that yoga can bestow us disease-free health and helps us to keep our biological, emotional and mental control well and it may also be helpful in enhancing longevity. *So Yogic way is the way of life.*

This modern world is having a lifestyle which is only centralised towards work professionalism and work proficiency. Due to this, human beings of this modern era have become completely profession oriented and haved become the warehouse of stress-related diseases which are either physical stress or mental stress, thereby causing neuro-physiological disorders or completely psychiatric disorders. Then begins their journey beings to doctors who either give medicines to control the symptoms of the disease or the clinical psychologists who give counselling which works as a further dent to the psyche of the patient because neither medicine nor counselling is anytime able to deliver complete cure to the patient due to the simple reason that none of these modern therapies or their practitioners have any methodology to dissolve the core cause of the evolution of such diseases in a particular patient.

Now the question arises that how come Yoga comes into the role of this problem? The answer to this question is very simple. If you refer to the chapter-1 (What is Yoga?) of this book you will again realise that the Yoga philosophy is a part of the six-fold philosophy of the evolutionary system of human life in relation to the whole cosmos, relating man as a *miniature universe*. Now the Yoga philosophy says that the whole universe is composed of *eternal primordial material* which is nothing else but waves and this primordial material is actually the *cosmic psyche*. So if we relate to the Yoga philosophy, then we can realise that man is a miniature universe and hence, whatever is the property by virtue of the universe, the same will be reflected in human beings as well. The environment surrounding the person has the major effect in causing stress and in turn this stress causes the other malfunctions in the person's system pertaining to physical or psychological issues. The Yoga methodology helps the person to attune his or her own nervous system in such a way that the electro-chemical discharge in one's nervous system behaves like a single gigantic battery which annihilates those pulses in the nervous system which are the cause for the stress on the diseased organs or the system of the body. *Hence, the Yoga methodology starts seizing the core cause of the stress which becomes the cause behind the disease in any system or organ in human body.*

On the other hand, if we take the medicinal system of the modern medicinal therapy, such a system only suppresses the symptoms of the particular disease rather than elimination of the core cause of the stress which serves as a base platform for the disease(s). This in turn makes the person more stressed and sometimes causes multiple organ failure and becomes fatal in many cases.

Similarly, if we take the modern clinical psychological solutions, then in this case also, these psychologists only give counselling which merely serves as a thought diversion tool rather than eliminating the core cause which generates such thought patterns that cause those stress patterns and serve as a base platform for the disease(s). This kind of therapy also facilitates a damaging tool in the psyche and behavioural patterns of the patient because instead of eliminating the core cause of the stress waves which causes the disease rather providing the thought pattern changing tools, this can actually cause a shift to the natural pattern of the patient's psyche by turning and twisting it in some other direction. This can serve as a more harmful platform in which the person may completely damage his/her psyche.

In such above comparisons, the Yoga philosophy never allows or facilitates intervention of external material (the medicines) or the external thought wave patterns (external psyche patterns by the other person through counselling) into the patient's physical body or psyche system. Rather, the Yoga methodology helps and trains the patient to attune his or her own energy system as well as neuro-physiological system in order to vibrate the whole neuro-physiological system as well as energy system of one's body in one phase such that it becomes only one single-phased gigantic wave. This single-phasedgigantic wave then eliminates all other turbulent waves which were serving as the base platform for the different types of stress which in turn were becoming the cause for different diseases in the organs or systems of the body.

The result is that the patient is free from all types of stress and in turn completely cures from all types of diseases without any external intervention by foreign matter to one's body or foreign waves by someone else and no side effects on one's body or psyche thereby remaining the same individual from both the physical and mental aspect which is not in the case of the modern medicinal therapies and modern clinical psychological methodologies.

Hence, the core philosophy and methodology is the most holistic approach to the diseased mind as well as the body, and that too without any side effects on the mind or body and thus, the person is the same individual after being completely cured from the problems one was suffering.

That is why the *Yoga philosophy* and *methodology* is the *real holistic* one for all without any discretion.

Important points to remember

A Yoga Practitioner should be well versed in all Yogic techniques and eight limbs of Yoga. He should know in details certain Yoga tips for his knowledge as well as his application. Important Yoga tips are given below:

- *Yoga is not only limited to the body, it includes the body, mind and soul as well. To understand Yoga as a physical exercise is misleading.*
- *Yogasanas are actually the discipline of the physical body in the beginning. Asanas refer to a steady comfortable*

pose. "Sthiram Sukham Asanam".

- *Yogic saints have developed Asanas by referring to animals, birds, trees and other creatures in order to stretch or relax.*
- *Asanas should always be practised in a slow and relaxed manner.*
- *Remember Yoga is relaxation, not exertion.*
- *Each movement should be done with the co-ordination of the breath.*
- *Do not haste. Let your muscles and nerves take its own time to relax and stretch.*
- *Make Yogasana a regular practice each day.*
- *Always take help from a trained Yoga Teacher and do not practise it by reading books alone.*

Chapter 3

Surya Namaskar (Sun Salutation)

Introduction

Surya Namaskar, also known in English as *Sun Salutation* is a combined sequence of *Hatha Yoga Asanas.* The Practice of *Surya Namaskar* is very beneficial for our health and well-being. It balances and harmonises the *prana* throughout the body and thus revitalises your whole body. Its effects are experienced on three levels, i.e., the Body, Mind and the Soul. This practice maintains a steady state of these three keeping the body in perfect health. There are 12 steps in this technique. To begin with, please stand erect with your legs together. Also bring the palms together in *namaskar mudra*. Now practise as explained in the following steps.

Step 1 (Pranamasana) — Invoke

- ☞ To begin with, please stand erect with your legs together. Also bring the palms together in the *namaskar mudra.*

Step 2 (Hasta Uttanasana) — Intent/Inhale

☞ Take your hands above the head while inhaling and bend the trunk backward.

Step 3 (Hastapadasana) — Surrender/Exhale

☞ Bend your body forward while exhaling. Touch the forehead to the knees. Also keep the palms on the floor on either side of your feet.

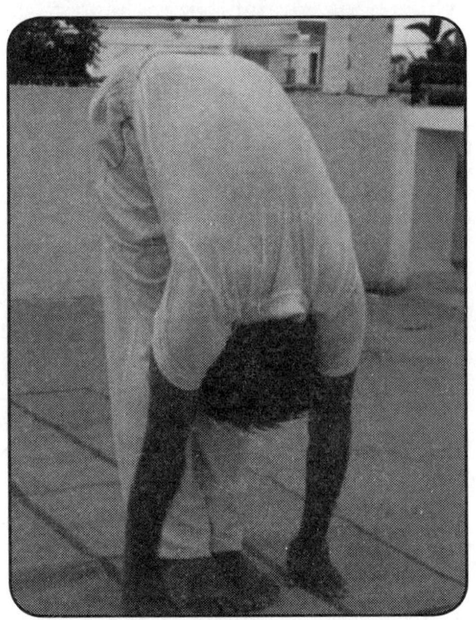

Step 4 (Aekpaadprasarnaasana) – Assume/Inhale

☞ Now take breath in and kick the right leg back. Push your buttock forward and downward so that the left leg is perpendicular to the ground. Now look up.

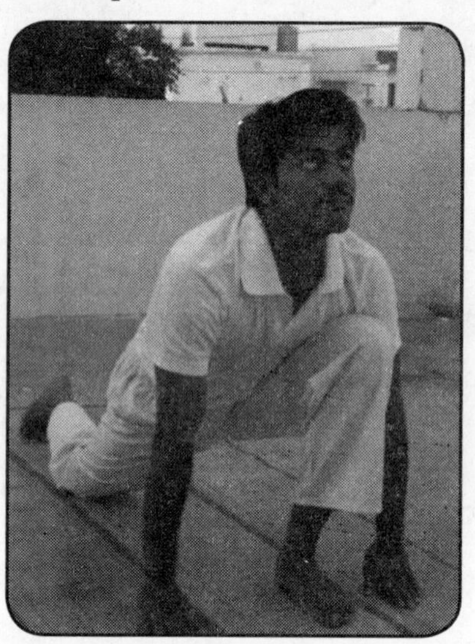

Step 5 (Chaturanga Dandasana) – Align/Exhale

☞ Now exhale and take the left leg back, resting only on palms and toes. Keep the body straight from head to toes inclined to the ground at about 30°.

☞ Keep your neck in line with the back.

Step 6 (Ashtanga Namaskara) – Awareness/Inhale

- ☞ While inhaling now, bend the legs at the knees and rest them on the floor with buttocks resting on the heels. Don't alter the position of your palms and toes.
- ☞ Exhale as you rest the forehead on the floor.
- ☞ Now relax in normal breathing.

Step 7 (Bhujangasana) – Surge-Upward/Exhale

- ☞ Inhale and raise your head and trunk making the spine concave upwards without lifting the position of the hands and feet.
- ☞ Arch the back as far as you can until the elbows are straight.
- ☞ Keep the knees off the ground.

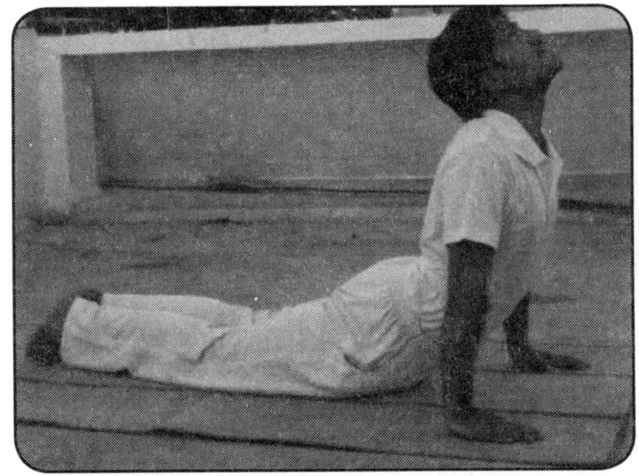

Step 8 (Adho Mukha Savasana) — Expand as Space Inhale/Exhale

☞ While exhaling, raise the buttocks and push the head down until the heels touch the ground without shifting the position of the hands and feet.

Step 9 (Ashwa Sanchalanasana) — Ignite/Inhale

☞ Inhale and bring the right leg in between the two hands. Arch the back concave upwards as in step 3 until the right leg is perpendicular to the ground.

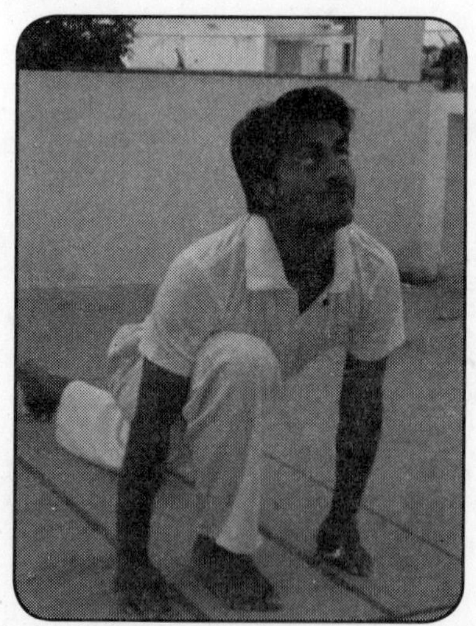

Step 10 (Uttanasana) – Void/Exhale

☞ Exhale and bring your left foot forward next to the right foot and reach down with your upper body to touch the forehead to the knees as in step 2.

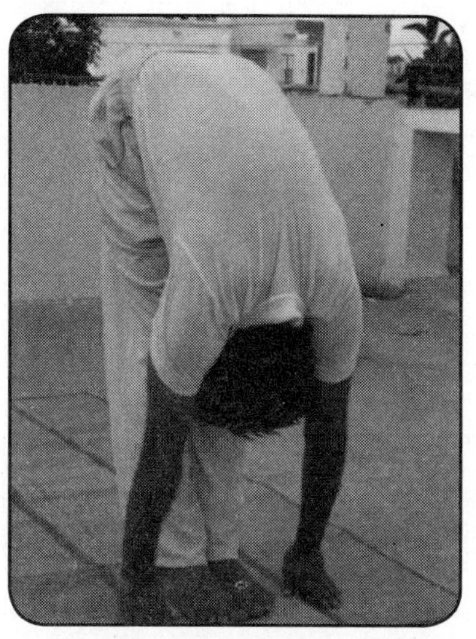

Step 11 (Hasta Uttanasana) – Fullness/Inhale

☞ Take your hands above the head while inhaling and bend the trunk backward.

Step 12 (Pranamasana) — Third Eye/Exhale

- ☞ While inhaling, come up to your original position.
- ☞ This completes one round of SURYA NAMASKAR. Repeat this practice up to three rounds.

Minimum Rounds

One round of Sun Salutation consists of two sequences, the first leading with the right foot in positions, 4 and 9, and the second leading with the left. Hands must be in one place from positions, 3 to 10 and movements should match with the breathing. It is good to start by practising four rounds and gradually build up to twelve rounds.

The description of *mantra* and corresponding *chakras* and *asanas* are also given in the following table :

Sl. No.	Mantra	Chakra	Asana
1.	Om Mitraya Namah	Anahata	Pranamasana
2.	Om Ravaye Namah	Vishuddhi	Hasta Uttanasana
3.	Om Suryaya Namah	Swadhisthana	Hastapaadasana
4.	Om Bhanave Namah	Ajna	Aekpaadprasarnaasana
5.	Om Khagaya Namah	Vishuddhi	Chaturanga Dandasana
6.	Om Pushpe Namah	Manipura	Ashtanga Namaskara

7.	Om Hiranya Garbhaya Namah	Swadhisthana	Bhujangasana
8.	Om Maricaye Namah	Vishuddhi	Adho Mukha Svanasna
9.	Om Adityaya Namah	Ajna	Ashwa Sanchalanasana
10.	Om Savitre Namah	Swadhisthana	Uttanasna
11.	Om Arkaya Namah	Vishuddhi	Hasta Uttanasana
12.	Om Bhaskaraya Namah	Anahata	Pranamasana

General Instruction

- *Surya Namaskar* should be practised in the morning before breakfast in empty stomach or in the evening.
- *Surya Namaskar* is always preferred facing the direction of the rising sun (east) in the morning and setting sun (west) in the evening.
- In twelve steps of *Surya Namaskar,* you can count 5 seconds for each step. It means that one *Surya Namaskar* goes for about 1 minute.
- *Shavasana* should be practised at the end of the practice for rest.

Benefits of Surya Namaskar

- It activates the *chakras*.
- It balances imbalance of the *Vatta, Kapha* and the Pitta.
- It activates digestion and gets rid of constipation.
- It strengthens abdominal muscles.
- It ventilates the lungs, and oxygenates the blood.
- It tones up the nervous system and improves memory.
- It promotes sleep, calms tension and anxiety.
- Improves muscle flexibility.
- Prevents loss of hair and graying.
- Helps to reduce fat.
- Lends grace and ease of movements to the body.
- Broadens chest and beautifies arms.
- Makes the spine and waist flexible.
- Produces health, strength, efficiency and longevity.
- It helps us in our spiritual progress.

Chapter 4

Asanas

Introduction to Asanas

Various Asanas of Supine Pose

Supine Pose

- Lay comfortable on the floor in face up position.
- Body should align in a straight line.
- Feet together, hands touching the sides of the body resting on the floor, with the palm facing up.

Asanas from Supine Pose

1. Uttana Padasana: (Stretched Leg Pose)

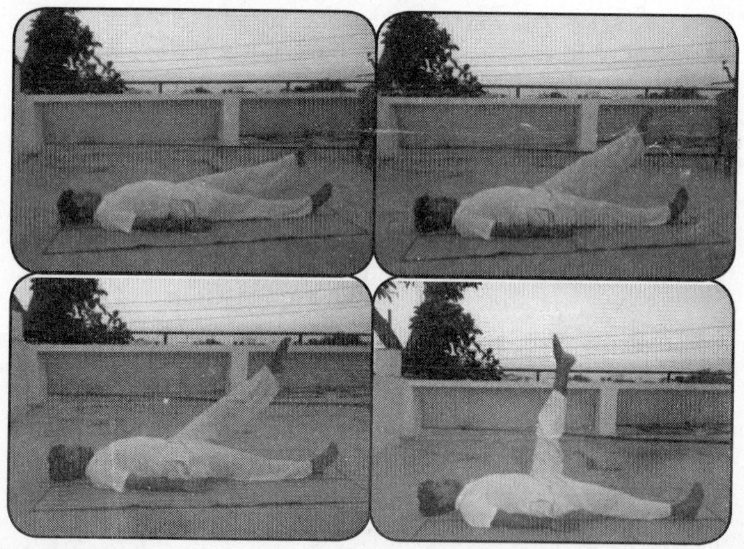

☞ **Single Leg**

Steps:

(a) Inhaling lift your left leg by up to 30 degrees.

(b) Toes pointed, feet stretched in front .

(c) Try not to bend the knee.

(d) Slowly raise to 45 degrees, then 60 degrees and then 90 degrees.

In the Asanas:

- Concentrate on your hip joints, thighs, knee, calf and feet
- Keep normal breathing.

Releasing the Pose:

- Exhale and slowly bring your left leg on the floor.
- Duration : 30 secs. – 45 secs. – 1 min.

Repeat with the right leg.

Double Leg Stretched Pose

Steps:

(a) Raise both legs together in this pose.

(b) Refer Steps Uttanpadasana single leg.

Benefits:

- Helps to strengthen the muscles of the abdomen and perinial muscles.
- It strengthens the lower back and pelvic.
- Helps to tone the hips, pelvic and thighs.

2. Pawana Muktasana (Wind Release Pose)

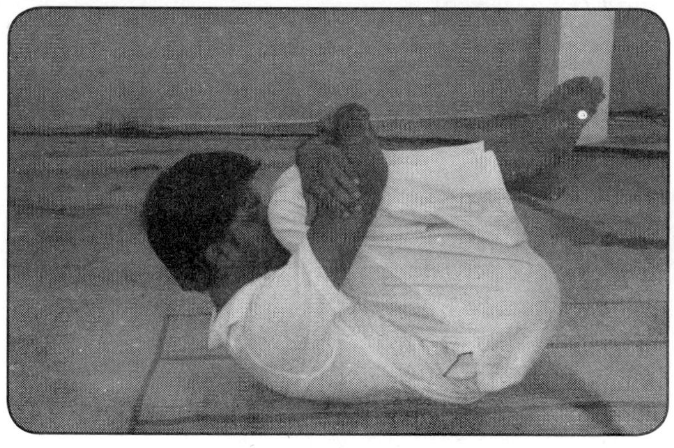

Steps :

(a) Bend the right leg in the knee, as shown.

(b) Bring the knee close to the chest by holding it by interlocking your fingers.

(c) Inhale deeply and then holding your breath lift your head up and try to touch the nose with the knee.

In the Asanas:

- Concentrate on your belly, neck and spine.
- Keep normal breathing.

Releasing the Pose :

- Exhale slowly and return to the initial pose.
- Now repeat it with the left leg.
- *Pawana Muktasana* should then be practised by bending both the legs together. Rest follow the same procedure of the single leg.
- Duration: 30 secs. to 1 min.

Benefits:

- Effective in removing wind and constipation.
- It renders a beneficial massage to the pelvis and abdominal muscles.
- Useful in treatments of impotence, sterility and menstrual problems.

Limitations :

People with severe pelvic and spinal problems must avoid this pose.

3. Naukasana (Boat Pose)

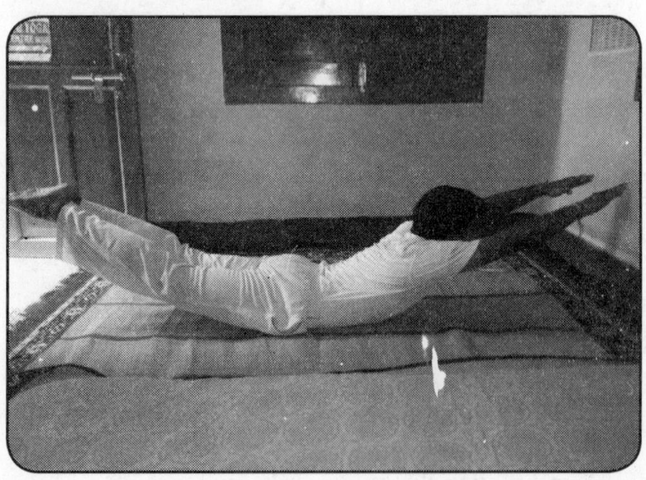

Steps:

(a) Inhale deeply

(b) Retain your breath and start raising your head, shoulders, arms, trunk and legs together off the ground.

(c) The body should rest on your buttocks.

(d) Keep your spine straight.

In the Asana:

- Breathing normal.
- Concentrate on the tension created on the muscles of the body, especially the abdomen.

Releasing the Pose:

- Exhale slowly and retuın to the supine pose.
- Duration: 30 secs. to 1 min.

Benefits:

- It rejuvenates the body and completely refreshes the mind and body after you release the pose.
- Works almost on all the systems and organs of the body.

4. Chakrasana (Wheel Pose)

Steps:

(a) Place your palms behind the shoulders. The fingers should point the shoulders.

(b) Keep a gap of 30 cm between the feet and the knee. Bend your knees and bring the heels so that they touch the buttocks.

(c) Inhaling lift your body upwards arching your back.

(d) Strengthens the arms and legs.

(c) Keep your eyesight between the palms.

In the Asana:

- Practise relaxed and slow breathing.
- Concentrate on wrists, palms, spine, lower back, pelvic region and feet.

Releasing the Pose:

- Exhale slowly and lower the body in such a way that the head rests front on the floor and then the whole body.
- Duration: As comfortable as you feel.

Benefits:

- Stimulates the hormonal secretions of the body.
- Removes blockages of the spine and strengthens the spinal cord and the spinal muscles.
- It relieves gynaecological disorders.

Limitations:

- If you are feeling weak, do not practise *Chakrasana*.
- If you have weak wrist, lower back and severe spinal problems, don't practise it.

5. Halasana (Plough Pose)

Steps:

(a) Raise both the legs up and bring them to make a 90 degree.

(b) Support your back by placing on the arms to the sides of the lower back.

(c) Raise roll your back and bring your feet close to the floor. Keep your legs straight.

(d) If possible, place your feet on the floor. This completes the *Halasana*.

In the Asana:

- Concentrate on the spine the upper back, the neck and the abdomen.

Releasing the Pose:

- Exhaling bring your back slowly on the floor.
- The legs will automatically come to a 90-degree angle.
- Slowly place your legs on the floor.
- Duration: 15 secs. to 1 min.

Benefits:

- It activates the digestion process.
- Helps to relieve constipation.
- Spleen and suprarenal glands get revitalised. Hence, promotes the secretion of insulin by the pancreas.
- Improves the liver and kidney functions.
- Balances the metabolic rate and boosts the immune system.
- Strengthens the abdominal muscles.
- Improves blood circulation.

Limitation:

- Should not be practised by people suffering from arthritis of the neck (Spondylitis, Spondolysis)
- Any severe back injury (slipped disc)
- Hernia, Sciatica and High Blood Pressure.

6. Viprit Karni (Inverted Pose)

Steps:

(a) Assume the pose of *Halasana*. Keep the feet above the floor.

(b) Place your palm on the sides of the lower back to support the hips and carry the weight of the body.

(c) Now raise your legs up keeping the knee and feet together. The toes should be pointed upwards.

(d) The trunk of the body will remain at 45 degrees.

In the Asana:

- Body weight is on the shoulder with the support of neck and head.
- Keep your gaze on the toes.

Releasing Pose:

- Exhale slowly and lower the legs towards the head.
- Bring your back slowly on the floor.
- Now slowly place your legs on the floor.
- Duration: 15 secs. – 30 secs. – 1 min – 3 mins. – 5 mins.

Benefits:

- It is a preparatory practice for *Sarvangasana.*
- Helps remove the stagnant blood from the lower body.
- Those who cannot do *Sarvangasana*, may benefit from *Viprit Karni.*

7. Sarvangasana (Shoulder Stand Pose)

Steps:

(a) Assume *Halasana* with the legs, a bit off the floor.

(b) Support your back by placing the palms to the back of the ribcage aside the spine.

(c) In this pose, the chin is locked with the collar bone which is required in the final pose of *Sarvangasana*.

(d) Raise your legs to the vertical position.

(e) Legs and trunks will be in a straight line.

In the Asana:

- Gaze at the toes.
- Then close your eyes and relax.

Releasing the Pose:

- Exhale slowly and lower the legs towards the heads.
- Bring your back slowly on the floor.
- Now slowly place your legs on the floor.
- Duration: As comfortable as possible.

Benefits:

- Improving the circulation of the neck region which improves the condition of the eyes, ears and throat. Helps to remove the tonsils and nose ailments.
- Boosts the immune system.
- Removes anxiety, fear and depression.
- Removes the stagnant blood from the legs, abdomen and the reproductive organs.

- Most helpful in thyroid problems.
- Effective in varicose veins.

Limitations:

- High Blood Pressure
- Cervical Spondylitis
- Enlarged Spleen, Liver and Thyroid
- Thrombosis or Impure Blood
- Weak Eye Muscles
- Slipped Disc
- Heart Ailments
- During Menstruation
- Advance Stage of Pregnancy

8. Matsyasana (Fish Pose)

Note : This *asana* should be practised after *Sarvangasana.*

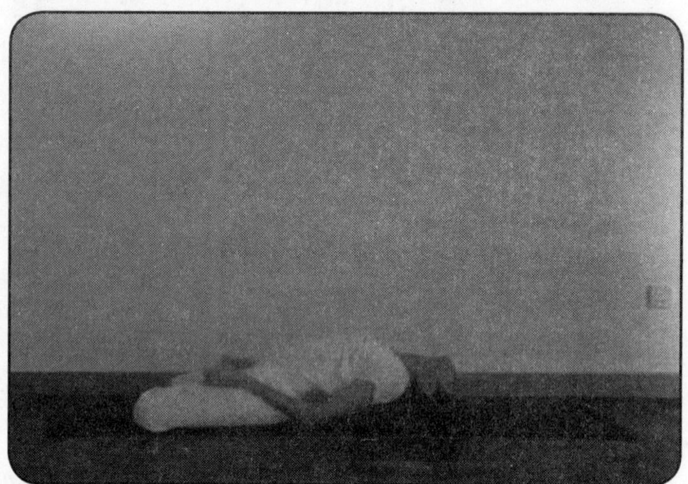

Steps:

- Sitting in *Padmasana.* Slowly take the help of your elbows to lie down on the back.
- Slowly lie down on your back completely.
- Now take the help of the elbows or palms and bend your head backward placing the middle of the head on the ground.
- Catch hold the toes with your index finger and place the elbows on the ground.

Releasing the Pose:

- Now returning to the original position, release the toes and taking the help of the hands straighten the head.
- Duration: Practise it 1/3rd of the time taken in the *Sarvangasana*.

Benefits :

- This *asana* increases the benefits of the *Sarvangasana.*

9. Ashwini Mudra (Horse Pose)

Steps:

- Assume the *Sarvangasana.*
- Now bend both the knees and bring them to your forehead.
- Try to relax and contract, and again relax the anal sphincter muscles.

In the Asana:

- Keep the whole concentration in your practice.
- Beware of the perineum region.

Releasing the Pose:

- Come to *Sarvangasana.*
- Follow the steps to release the pose of *Sarvangasana.*

Benefits:

- For fit body
- For anti-ageing

10. Shavasana (Corpse Pose)

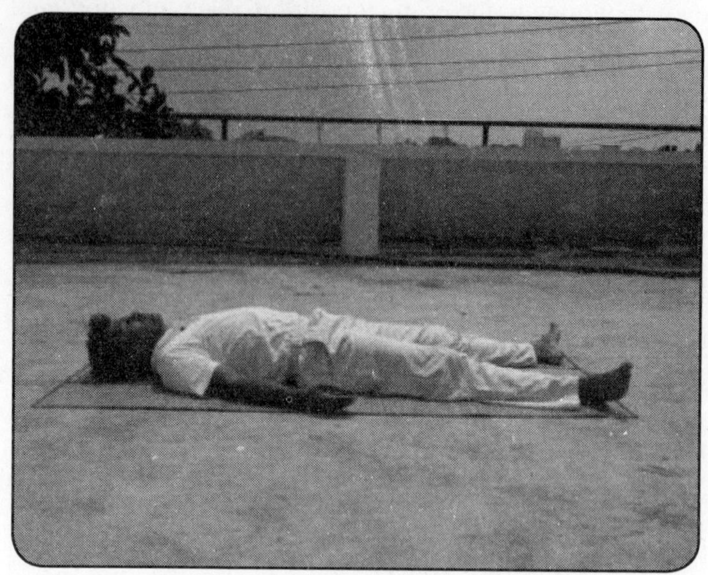

Steps:

(a) Bring your legs apart from each other.

(b) Heels joining the inside of the toes outside.

(c) Hands by the sides of the body.

(d) Palms facing up.

(e) Relax your whole body as if you have no control on your body.

(f) The Lie as if your body is lifeless.

(g) Close your eyes and relax.

In the Pose:

- First concentrate on the closed eyes.
- Then on the region of the third eye.
- Now try to concentrate on each and every part of the body – one by one.
- You may concentrate on the *chakras*.
- Beware of your breath throughout the practice.

Note:

- *Shavasana* must be practised after each and every pose.

- Only after *Shirshasana,* first do *Tadasana* and then double the time of *Shirshasana* and Shavasana.

Prone Lying Pose

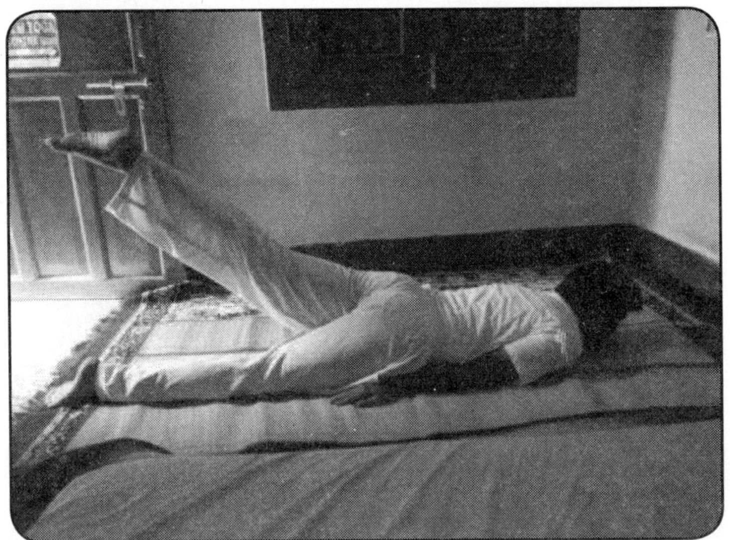

- Lie on the mat with face down.
- Place your chin on the mat.
- Hands by the sides of the body, anr the palms facing down.
- Knee and feet together. Feet flat on the mat.
- The whole body should be aligned in a straight line, from the trunk till the toe.

Asanas of Prone Lying Pose

1. Shalabhasana (The Locust Pose)

Steps:

(a) Inhale and lift the left leg off the floor.

(b) The lift should be done with a straight leg, and it should not bend in the knee.

In the Pose:

- Concentrate on the lower abdomen.
- Also on the inner thighs, calf and feet.
- The abdominal organs get a nice massage but always remain care ful of this area.

Releasing the Pose:

- Exhale slowly and bring the leg to the floor.
- Repeat with the right leg too.

2. Shalabhasana (Double Leg)

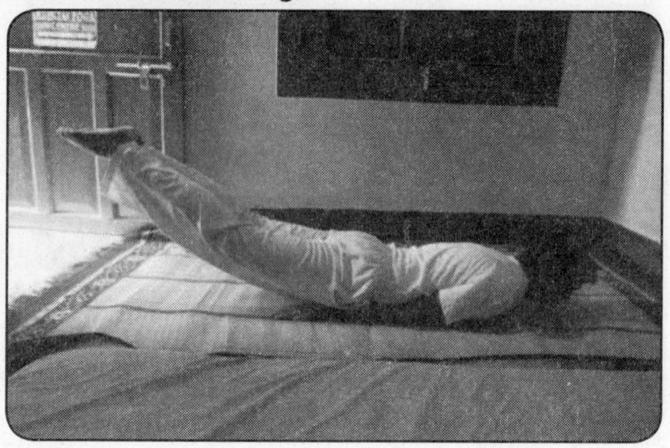

Steps:

(a) Keep both the knees and feet in touch with each other.

(b) Bring the palms underneath the hips (inner thighs).

(c) Keep your palms down placed on the floor.

(d) Inhale and lift both the legs.

(e) The Lumbar will hold the position in the final pose.

In the Pose:

- Concentrate on the Lumbar region.
- Take breath in a normal way.
- Remain aware of the thighs.

Releasing the Pose:

- Slowly exhale and lower the legs, placing on the mat.
- Bring your palms to the sides of the body.
- Duration: 15 secs. – 10 secs. – 15 secs. – 30 secs.

Benefits:

- Beneficial for those suffering from backaches, sciatica etc.
- Slipped disc.
- Strengthens the lower back and abdominal muscles.

- Stimulates the autonomous nervous system.

Limitations:

- Weak heart, high blood pressure
- Peptic Ulcer
- Hernia
- Intestinal Tuberculosis

3. Bhujangasana (Cobra Pose)

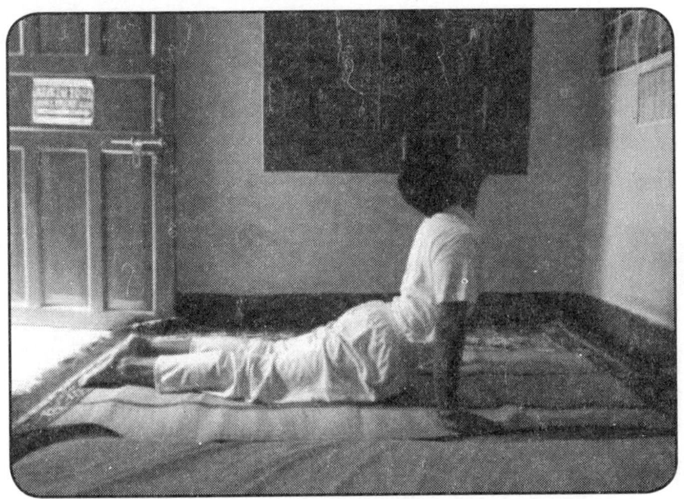

Steps:

(a) Place your palms on the sides of the shoulder.

(b) Inhaling first lift your head up from the neck.

(c) Keep raising by lifting the upper back and trunk.

- Now straighten the hands.
- Keep the shoulders expanded and the head back.
- If possible, keep the navel touched to the mat.

In the Pose:

- Concentrate on the third eye.
- Fill the strengthening of the spinal muscles.
- Concentrate on the lower back and wrists.

Releasing the Pose:

- Exhale slowly and bring the abdomen on the floor. Then bend your hands at the elbow.

- Now place the chest and then the forehead on the floor.
- Bring your hands by the sides of the body and the chin on the mat.
- Duration: 10 secs. – 15 secs – 30 secs. – 45 secs – 60 secs

Benefits:

- **Slipped disc:** When we get old, our back begins to hunch. This *asana* keeps the back straight, thus maintaining the flexibility and health of the spine.
- Tones the ovaries and uterus, pelvic muscles and the lower back muscles.
- Alleviate the problems of menstruation and gynaecological disorders.
- Improves digestion and removes constipation.
- Health of liver and kidneys improved.

Limitations:

- Hernia
- Peptic ulcers
- Intestinal tuberculosis
- Weak, diseased and ill persons

Note: This asana can be done without the support of hands. Them it has more profound effects.

4. Viprit Naukasana (Opposite Boat Pose)

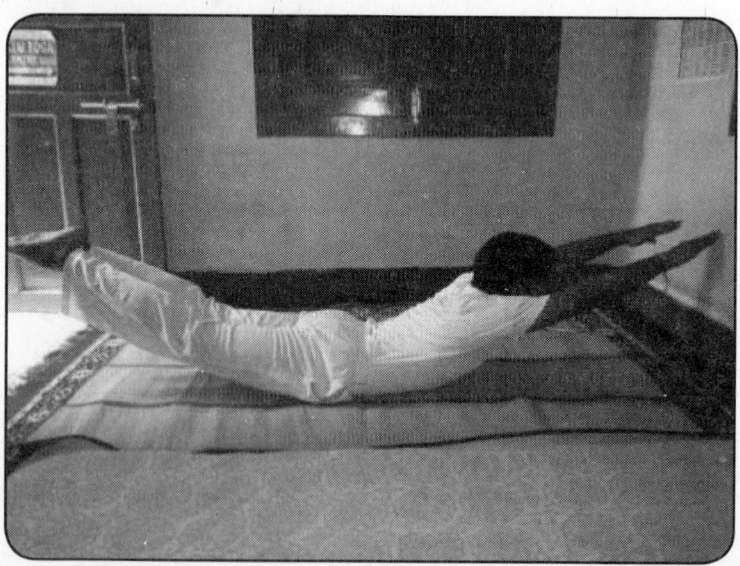

Steps:

- Stretch your hands to the front above the head and place the palms on the floor.
- Inhale and raise arms, your shoulders, legs together at the same time.
- The body will be resting on the abdomen in the final pose.

In the Pose:

- Concentrate on the posterior part of your body.
- Keep normal breathing.

Releasing the Pose:

- Exhale and slowly lower the whole body on the mat.
- Bring your hands by the side of the body.
- Duration: 5 secs. – 10 secs. – 15 secs. – 30 secs.

Benefits:

- Stretches and strengthens the muscles of the posterior part of the body.
- Thyroid and thymus glands are stimulated.
- The diaphragm gets a nice effect in this posture.
- Backache is also relieved.
- Tones the whole body, especially the upper back, the lower back, thighs and calves.

Limitations:

- Same as *Bhujangasana*

5. Dhanurasana (Bow Pose)

Steps:

- Start bending your legs in the knee, and bring the heels close to the hips from upwards.
- Catch the ankles from the sides.
- Place the forehead on the mat.
- Now inhale and raise the body upward by pulling the legs with the hands.
- The head will be upward and your gaze should be in the front.
- In the final pose, the body looks like a bow.

In the Asana:

- Keep normal breathing.
- Contract and tense the muscles of the back and lower back and the hips.
- Concentrate on the pose of the body which has become like a bow.

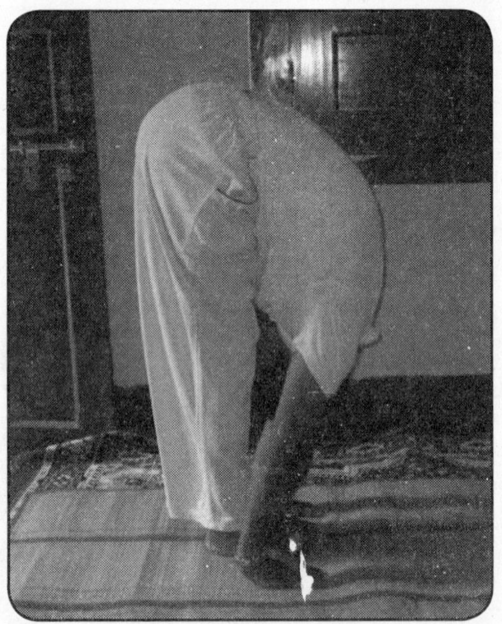

Releasing the Pose

- Exhale slowly and lower the body and the legs.
- Place the forehead on the mat.

- Release your hands and place by the sides of the body.
- Bring the feet back on the mat.
- Duration: 5secs. – 10 secs. – 15 secs. – 30 secs. – 1 min.

Benefits:

- Strengthens the muscles of the legs, neck, abdomen and the spine.
- Provides massage to the abdominal organs.
- Removes sluggishness of the liver and kidneys.
- Helps to remove the gastrointestinal disorders.
- Chronic constipation.
- Gives all the benefits of *Bhujangasana*.

Limitations:

- Same as *Bhujangasana*.
- Also those suffering from duodenal ulcers.

6. Makarasana (Crocodile Pose)

Steps:

(a) Stretch both the arms above the head and then fold from the elbows.

(b) Place one palm upon the another.

(c) Place the head on any side on the palms as comfortable, making the folded hands as a pillow.

In the Pose:

- Remain aware to the breath.
- Experience the calmness achieved during the *asana*.

  Note: The *asana* should be practised after all the poses in a lying pose.

Benefits:

- This is beneficial in asthma.
- Abdominal muscles get a massage.

Limitations:

1. Those having obesity, gas or high blood pressure and heart problems should not practise it.

Standing Pose

1. Stand erect with your legs together.
2. The body should align in a straight line.

3. The palms should be by the side of the body. The palms must touch the thighs to the sides.

Asanas in Standing Pose

1. Tadasana (The Palm Tree Pose)

Steps:

(a) Inhaling stretch the back, shoulder and chest upwards together with the arms stretching and raising above the head. Hands should be parallel to each other.

(b) Continue inhaling and lift the heels coming up onto the toes.

In the Asana:

- Do not lose the balance of the body.
- Stretch the entire body.
- Hold the breath in the final pose if doing for a short duration and normal breathing, if doing for a longer duration.

Releasing the Pose:

- Exhaling slowly bring the heels on the mat and the hands by the sides of the body.

Duration:

- One may repeat 5 rounds of shorter duration or hold the position for 1 to 3 minutes.

Benefits:

- Stretches the entire spinal muscles right from where it originates.
- Helps tone up the entire body.
- Stretches the abdominal rectus muscles.
- Excellent posture to develop concentration.
- Useful to practise after waking up from sleep to stimulate the muscles and nerves.
- Useful in developing physical and mental balance.

Limitations:

- There is no such limitation.
- Only if you had a recent fracture (within 3-4 months)

Hastapadasana (Forward Bending, Palm to Feet Pose)

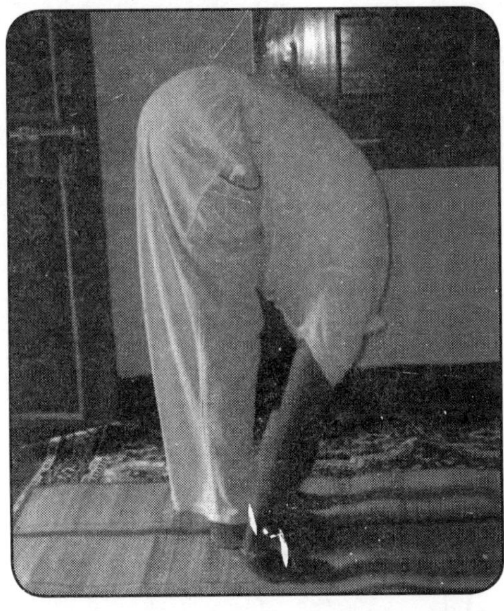

Steps:

(a) Inhaling lift hands up stretching the entire back muscles.

(b) Exhale and bend forward from the waist bringing the palms to the either side of the feet.

(c) Try to touch the knee with the forehead.

In the Asana:

- Keep breathing, but relaxed, slow and normal breathing.

- One may contract the abdominal muscles for a few seconds to achieve better forward bend.
- Try not to bend the leg in the knee.
- Concentrate on the pelvic region.

Releasing the Pose:

- Inhale and start slowly to raise your arms and the body from the waist.
- Exhaling, bring the hands by the sides of the body.

Duration:

- One may start from 10 seconds initially and then increase up to one minute.

Benefits:

- Removes flatulence.
- Strengthens the spinal nerves and muscles.
- Removes constipation.
- Strengthens the thigh, pelvic and calf muscles.

Limitations:

- People with severe back pain must not force the posture.
- They must practise half bend from the hips.

Vrikshasana (Tree Pose)

Steps:

(a) Fold the right leg in the knee and place the heel on the left groin sideways. The right feet toes should face downwards.

(b) The right knee must be perpendicular to the left leg.

(c) Inhaling, raise your arms up over the head and join the palms in a *Namaskar mudra*.

(d) Stretch the back, shoulder and waist upwards.

In the Asana:

- The balance should be maintained on the left leg.
- Your left leg should be straight and should not bend in the knee.
- Gaze to any particular point and remain aware of your breathing.

Releasing the Pose:

- Exhaling, bring your hands down by the sides of the body.
- Place the left leg at the side of the right leg on the mat.
- Repeat this with the other leg.

Duration:

- One may hold the position for as long as possible and should gradually increase the time to one minute.

Benefits:

- *Vrikshasana* strengthens the ligaments of feet, tendons and arches.
- Rheumatism patients can benefit by alleviating the pain.
- Improve the coordination of neuromuscular functions of the body.
- Helps to improve deep concentration and sense of balance.

Limitations:

- There is no such limitation.
- Only if had a recent fracture (within 3-4 months).

Garudasana (Eagle Pose)

Steps:

(a) Bend your legs at the knee and lift your right foot off the ground.

(b) Balancing your body on your left foot, place the right foot around the calf of the left leg.

(c) Press the left foot on the ground so that the right foot comfortably fits around to the left calf.

(d) Cross your arms at the elbow, the left hand over the right in front of the chest.

(e) Bend your elbows so that the fingers are pointing upwards and press the back of the hands against each other.

In the Asana:

- Twist your forearms further and try to bring both the palms facing each other.
- Place the fingers of the right hand in the palm of your left hand at the root of the thumb.
- Press the palms together as much as possible and lift your elbows until they are at level with your shoulders.
- Keep your breathing normal.

Releasing the Pose:

- Slowly unwind the hands and palms.
- Release the lock of the right foot against the left calf.
- Stand erect.
- Repeat the same with your legs and hands in reverse positions.

Duration:

- One may practise it for 15 seconds and increase up to one minute.

Benefits:

- Improves the flexibility of arms, shoulders, hip joints and thighs.
- Keeps the knee healthy.
- Improves the sense of balance.

Limitations:

- Persons suffering from knee or ankle pain.

Virasana

Steps:

(a) Place the feet on the mat and take the left leg to the back.

(b) Inhaling raise your arms up and join hands in a *namaskar* posture.

(c) Exhaling, bend the right leg in the knee. The right knee should be at 90 degrees from the floor.

(d) Inhaling, bend backwards from the trunk and waist.

In the Asana:

- Keep the balance of the body. Concentrate on the foot.
- Be aware of the entire body, especially the posterior part.
- Keep normal breathing.

Releasing the Pose:

- Exhaling, keep the upper body straight.
- Straighten the right leg at the knee.

- Release the *namaskar* posture and bring the hands to the sides of the body.
- Bring your left leg towards the right leg. The feet should touch each other.
- Repeat the posture with the other leg too!

Duration:

- As comfortable in the beginning, then up to one minute.

Benefits:

- Strengthens the entire back.
- Effective in cervical and lumbar spondilitis.
- Strengthens the hip muscles and thighs.
- Improves breathing by removing lung congestions.
- Brings confidence.

Limitations:

- High blood pressure
- Cardiovascular problems
- History of stroke, fainting, epilepsy
- Serious knee and lower back pain

Trikonasana (Triangle Pose)

Steps:

(a) Take your legs approximately a metre apart.

(b) Now bring your hands horizontally at the shoulder level.

(c) Fold the left leg in the knee up to 90 degrees.

(d) Place the left palm on the floor in front of the left feet.

(e) The right hand should be vertical from the shoulder and the gaze set on the fingers.

In the Asana:

- Concentrate on the muscles of the stretched leg.
- Keep the hands in a vertical line from the shoulders.

Releasing the Pose:

- Bring the hands horizontal raising the upper body.
- Straighten the left leg in the knee
- Bring the legs and feet together.
- Repeat with the other side.

Duration:

- 30 seconds to one minute.

Benefits:

- Realigns displaced spinal discs.
- Removes arthritis of the lower back and dorsal region.
- Strengthens the back muscles.
- Corrects hunch shoulders, knee pain and flat feet.

Limitations:

- Do not practise if you are ill, are epileptic, have low blood pressure, migraine and headache.
- Do not practise if you have heart problems and cervical spondylisis.
- Persons with weak lumbar must not practise this *asana*.

Parivrtta Trikonasana

Steps:

- Take your legs approximately a metre apart.
- Now bring your hands horizontally at the shoulder level.
- Fold the left leg in the knee up to 90 degrees.
- Twist from the trunk and waist and place the right palm on the floor in the back of the left feet.
- The left hand should be vertical from the shoulder and the gaze set on the fingers.

In the Asana:

- Concentrate on the muscles of the stretched leg.
- Feel the compression of the abdominal organs.
- Keep the hands in a vertical line from the shoulders.

Releasing the Pose:

- Straighten the trunk and waist, thus bringing the hands horizontal raising the upper body.
- Straighten the left leg in the knee.
- Bring the legs and feet together.
- Repeat the same with your legs and hands in reverse positions.

Duration:

- 30 seconds to one minute.

Benefits:

- All the benefits of *Trikonasana*.
- Improves the functioning of the abdominal muscles.
- Keeps the waist and belly in shape.

Limitations:

- Do not practise if you are ill, are epileptic, suffer from low blood pressure, migraine and headache.
- Do not practise if you have heart problems and cervical spondylisis.
- Persons with weak lumbar, duodenal ulcers and peptic ulcers, must not practise this *asana*.

Natrajasana (The King Dancer Pose)

Steps:

(a) Start raising the left leg up from the back by folding in the knee.

(b) Catch the ankle from outside with the left palm.

(c) Straighten the right hand up to 45 degree angle.

In the Asana:

- Concentrate on the feet and spine.
- Gaze should be at the front.
- Slow and relaxed breathing and maintain the balance.

Benefits:

- Develops poise and a graceful carriage.
- Tones and strengthens the leg muscles.
- Chest is expanded and shoulder blades get movements.
- The spine becomes healthy as all the vertebrae get a relief.
- Improves balance of the mind and the body.

Limitations:

- Serious back, knee, or neck injury.

Sitting Pose

Steps:

(a) Sit with your legs straight.

(b) Both the legs aligned together.

(c) Feet and knee to be in contact with each other.

(d) Hands by the sides of the body.

(e) Palms placed on the floor is such a way that the fingers should be pointing at the front.

Asanas in Sitting Pose

Janushirshasana (Head of the Knee Pose)

Steps:

(a) Fold the right leg in the knee and place the heel to the groin of the left leg.

(b) The knee should touch the floor.

(c) Inhale stretching the upper body above the waist lifting your arms.

(d) Exhale and bend from the waist.

(e) Catch the left feet or the big toe. Place the head touching to the right knee.

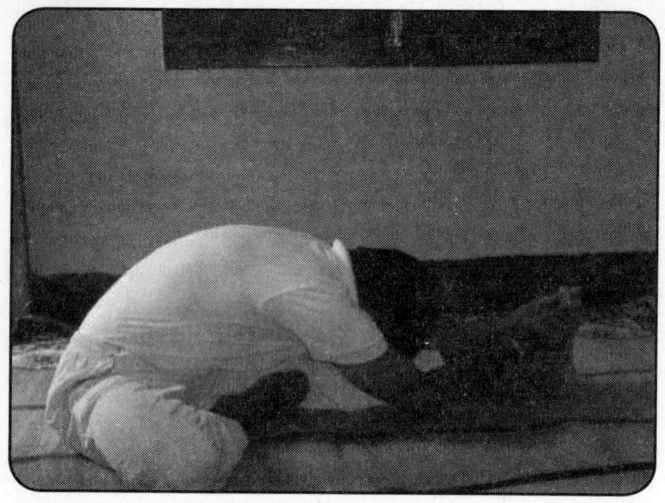

In the Pose:

- Relax and bend forward with each exhalation.
- The more you spend time in the pose, the more you gain flexibility.

Releasing the Pose:

- Inhale and release the hold of the feet. Lift your body from the waist up.
- Exhaling bring hands back to the sides of the body and palms on the floor.
- Repeat with the other leg too.

Duration: About 30 seconds in the beginning and then up to three minutes.

Benefits:

- Strengthens the calf, knee, thighs and the pelvic region.
- It is a preparatory practice for the posterior pose.
- Helps to open up the hip joint.

Limitations:

- Almost everyone can practise.
- People suffering from weaknesses and diarrhoea should not practise.

Paschimottanasana (Posterior Pose)

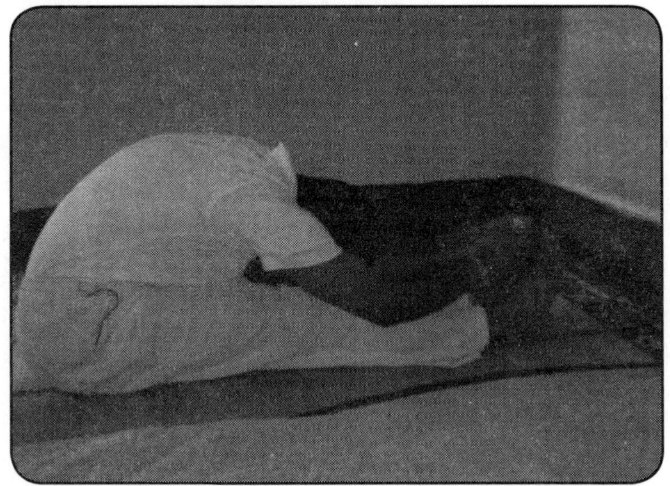

Steps:

(a) Inhale and stretch your arms.

(b) Exhaling, bend from the waist forward.

(c) Try to catch the big toes, place the elbows on the floor on both the sides and let the forehead touch the knee.

In the Pose:

- Relax and bend forward with each exhalation.
- The more you spend time in the pose, the more you gain flexibility.
- Concentrate on the spine and the movement of the abdomen.

Releasing the Pose:

- Inhale and release the hold of the feet. Lift your body from the waist up.
- Exhaling, bring your hands back to the sides of the body and palms on the floor.

Duration: 30 seconds in the beginning and then up to three minutes.

Benefits:

- Improves the health of the kidneys, liver, ovaries and the uterus.
- Very good for women.
- Menstrual difficulties can be cured.

- Stretches the neck, back, spine, hamstrings and calf.
- Diabetic patients can get benefit.
- Digestion problems are solved. Helps to keep the tummy flat.

Limitations:

- Weaknesses
- Diarrhoea
- Asthmatic patients
- Severe back problems

Vajrasana (Thunderbolt Pose)

Steps:

(a) Assume a kneel down position.

(b) Sit on your calf muscles, while your buttocks touch the heels and the big toes join each other.

(c) Keep your palm on the thigh or knee, wherever comfortable.

In the Pose:

- Keep normal breathing.
- Keep your concentration in your body, especially along the wind pipe and the third eye.

Releasing Pose:

- Bring the left leg straight and then right.
- Assume a sitting pose.

Benefits:

- During meditation, it is important to have the spine erect in the sitting pose. In this posture, it happens automatically; hence very good posture for meditation practice.
- This is the only posture that can be done after taking meals. It is effective and aides digestion.
- Improves the blood circulation in the pelvic region.
- It is associated with *Vajra nadi* and hence, it becomes a good posture for meditation practice.

Limitations:

- Generally, there is no limitation to do this pose, until unless one has severe pain in the knee or have stiff ankles.

Note: Those who feel numbness at the calf muscles need to practise the posture again and again to overcome the problem.

Swastikasana (Auspicious Pose)

Steps:

(a) Keep 1 to 1.5 feet distance between the legs.

(b) Bend the left leg in the knee and place the sole of the foot to the side of the thigh of the right leg.

(c) Now bend the right leg in the knee and place the foot between the calf and the thigh of the left leg.

(d) Place your palms on the knee.

In the Pose:

- Relax your mind and body.

- Keep the spine erect.
- Concentrate from the *root chakra* up to the *crown chakra*.

Releasing the Pose:

- Release the right leg first and straighten the leg.
- Release the left leg and straighten the leg.

Duration: Initially, 15 to 30 seconds, later 3 to 5 mins.

Benefits:

- The heart rate is relaxed.
- The pulse rate also gets relaxed.
- The functioning of the backbone improves.
- Effective for self-awareness.

Limitations:

- Simple and can be done by anybody.

Siddhasana (Male Accomplished Pose)

This *asana* is to be practised by males only.

Steps:

(a) Take 1 to 1.5 feet distance between the legs.

(b) Bend the left leg in the knee and place the heel touching the groin.

(c) Now bend the right leg and place the heel just on top of the left feet.

(d) The sole of the right foot should touch the left thigh.

(e) Hands to be kept on the knees.

In the Pose:

- Concentrate on the whole body and mind.

Releasing the Pose:

- Straighten the right leg.
- Straighten the left leg.

Duration: 3 to 5 mins.

Benefits:

- Beneficial for those who suffer from wet dreams.
- Increases the concentration.
- Excellent pose for meditative purpose.

Limitations:

- Anyone suffering from sciatica.
- Persons having problems related to the sacral portion of the body.

Siddha Yoni Asana (Female Accomplished Pose)

This *asana* should be practised by femalee only.

Steps:

(a) Take 1 to 1.5 feet distance between the legs.

(b) Bend the left leg in the knee and place the sole of the feet to the inner thigh of the right leg, the heel should press against the *labia majora* (the front of the Vagina).

(c) Now bend the right leg and place the foot on the calf of the left leg.

In the Pose:

- Concentrate on the body and mind.

Releasing the Pose:

- Straighten the right leg.
- Straighten the left leg.

Duration: 3 to 5 minutes.

Benefits:

- It has a direct influence on the nerve plexuses of the female reproductive system.
- Helps to keep the sexual organ healthy.
- Excellent posture for meditative practice for women as their root *chakra position* is slightly different than men.

Limitations:

- Anyone suffering from sciatica.
- Persons having problems related to the sacral portion of the body.

Padmasana (Lotus Pose)

Steps:

(a) Spread the legs to 1 and 15 feet distance.

(b) Fold the left leg in the knee and place the foot on the thigh, the heel of the foot should be close to the lower abdomen.

(c) Fold the other leg and place it on top of the opposite thigh.

In the Pose:

- Concentrate along the spine, the third eye throughout the duration in the pose.
- Both the knees should rest on the floor.
- Keep your hands either in a *Dhyan mudra* or the *Chin mudra*.

Releasing the Pose:

- Slowly release the right leg, straighten it and keep it on the floor.
- Slowly release the left leg, straighten the left leg and place it on the floor.

Duration: 3 mins – 5 mins and later, as much as you feel comfortable.

Benefits:

- Improves self-awareness.
- Calms the brain and the entire system.
- Improves flexibility of the hips, knees and calf.
- Increase the blood flow to the pelvic and the perineum.

Limitations:

- Persons suffering from sciatica, and sacral infections must not practice this pose.

Ardhamatseyndrasana (Half Spinal Twist Pose)

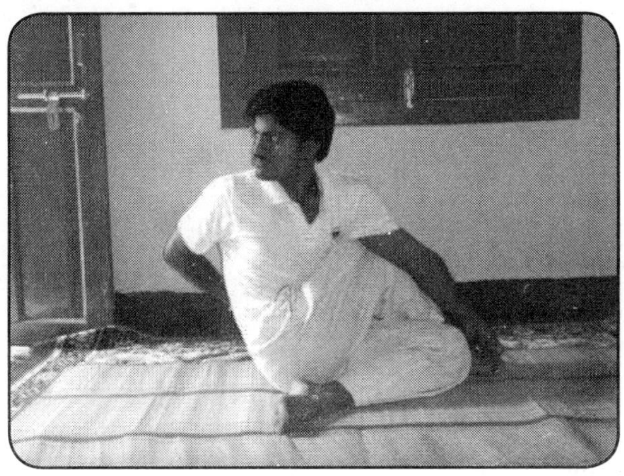

Steps:

(a) Fold the left leg in the knee and place the left feet on the side of the right knee on the floor. The knee should be at 90° angle to the feet.

(b) Fold the right leg and place the heel touching the left buttock.

(c) Lift the right hand upwards, twist the body from the waist and trunk moving the left shoulder to the left, now roll the elbow or the upper arm to the left knee and try catching the left toes or feet. In case catching the feet or toes is difficult, just try to touch the feet or legs.

(d) Expand your chest, the shoulders should be aligned in one line and fix your gaze backwards to the left.

In the Pose:

- Do not strain your eyes while looking back. Relax your eye balls keeping gaze straight.
- Spine should be erect.
- Achieve the final pose slowly and gradually.

Releasing the Pose:

- Move your head, shoulder and trunk towards the front.
- Release the lock of your hand and place the palm to the side of the body.
- Straighten the right leg and then the left leg on the floor.

Duration: Initially 30 secs each side and gradually increase this up to 3 mins each side.

Benefits:

- Excellent posture for those who suffer from sciatica, slipped disc and backache.
- Prevents the adjoining vertebrae to fuse together.
- Constipated people must twist first to the right and then to the left. This will help them get relief from constipation.
- The abdominal organs, muscles and the nerves remain in good health.

Limitations:

- People suffering from serious disease of the abdomen should not practise this *asana* e.g. hernia, peptic ulcer, hyperthyroidism, etc.
- Should not practise during pregnancy.
- People suffering from back problems must take extra care while practising this pose.

Shasankasana (Hare Pose)

Steps:

(a) Sit in Vajrasana.

(b) Bend forward from the waist.

(c) The upper body up to the chest from the waist should touch the thighs and the forehead should touch the floor.

(d) Your arms should rest on the floor above the head.

In the Pose:

1. Concentrate on the whole body. Do it part by part.
2. Spine, head, trunk and arms should be in a straight line.
3. The abdomen movement should be slow and relaxed in coordination with the breath.

Releasing the Pose:

1. Inhale and lift your upper body.
2. Assume Vajrasana.

   Duration: 3 to 5 mins

Benefits:

- Releases the pressure on the disc which keeps the vertebrae apart.
- Helpful in sciatica.
- The muscles and nerves soak in fresh blood as soon as the *asana* is released.

- Deep breathing gives massage to the abdominal organs.
- Calms the mind.

Marjariasana (Cat Pose)

Steps:

- Assume *Vajrasana*.
- Place the palms on the floor and lift the buttocks up. The legs from your knee to the hip should be vertical the while knees to the feet should be horizontal. Hands must be vertical to the shoulder.
- The distance between the knees to the hands will be exactly the measurement of the spine.
- Inhaling press your pelvic down and head upwards. Gaze upwards as much as you are comfortable.
- Exhaling, curve spine in the upward direction and bring your chin close to the centre of the shoulder blade.

Duration: 10 to 15 rounds.

Benefits:

- Keeps your spine supple.
- The nerves between the two vertebrae are relieved which gets squeezed between them.

Simhasana (Lion's Yawn Pose)

Steps:

(a) Assume *Vajrasana*.

(b) Separate the knees to a distance of 1 foot.

(c) Place the palms on the floor such that the fingers are pointed towards the body and the hands should be aligned to the centre of the body.

(d) Inhale deeply and then forcefully exhale taking your tongue out as much as possible. The tongue must point downwards, eyes should be half closed with your eyeballs gazing upwards.

In the Pose:

- Remain in the position as a long as you can breathe out.

Releasing the Pose

- Slowly relax your eyes and your take tongue inside.
- Release your hands and bring your knees together.
- Come back in a sitting pose.

Rounds: 5 to 10 times.

Benefits:

- An extra amount of carbon dioxide is removed from the lungs while you exhale.
- Strengthens the larynx, pharynx, parathyroid and thyroid glands. This helps for those who suffer from tonsillitis.
- Facial muscles get a good massage and thus, wrinkles do not appear on the face.

Limitations:

- No limitations. This can be done by everyone.

Sirshasana (Head stand pose)

Steps:

(a) Assume *Vajrasana.*

(b) Bend forward from the waist, fold the hands and place the elbows on the floor. Open the fold and interlock your fingers placing it on the floor.

(c) Support your head by placing occipital (back of the head) region touched to the palm.

(d) Lift the buttocks up; straighten the knee and the soles of your feet touching the floor.

(e) Bring your body straight from the head to the buttocks. Your spine should be erect.

(f) Bring the left knee close to the body folding the leg in the knee and the heels should come close to the buttocks. Then bring the right knee close to the body. The whole weight should now be on the head supported by the forearms and the elbows.

(g) Lift the knees to 90 degrees, but the legs should remain folded.

(h) Now straighten the legs.

In the Pose:

- Maintain the pressure of the body weight mainly on the head with the support of the forearms and the elbows.
- Keep the toes pointed or relaxed in the final pose as comfortable.
- Keep your eyes closed after, few days of practice.
- Keep the body in a straight line so that no pressure is on the neck.
- Maintain normal breathing.

Releasing the Pose:

- Start folding the legs in the knee, and the heels should touch the buttocks.
- Now bring the knee close to the body in the front.

- Straighten the legs and bring the toes on to the floor.
- Fold the leg in the knee and sit on your calf muscles.
- Assume *Vajrasana*.

Note: Practise *Tadasana* (Palm tree pose) after *Sirshasana*.

Chapter 5

Shatkarma (Body Purification Process)

One of the main practices in keeping the internal body healthy, clean and pure is 'Shatkarma'. Shatkarma is made of two Sanskrit words 'Shat' meaning six and 'Karma' meaning techniques or actions.

Yogi Swatmaram, 'a renowned Yogi' and the writer of *Hatha Yoga Pradapika*, states six purification processes.

We have tried here to give the practice of these *kriyas* in the following descriptions:

Neti

Referred to as *Nasal cleansing* or *Nasal wash* is basically done in two forms. One is *Jala Neti* and the second is *Sutra Neti*.

We will discuss *Jala Neti* as it is less complicated and easy than the *Sutra Neti*.

Process

The nasal passage is cleansed with purified lukewarm water and iodised salt which is poured through a *neti* or pot available in plastic or ceramic material.

Technique

Body position

- ☞ Hold the *neti* or the pot in the right hand and place the left palm on the left knee. This is to pour water from the right nostril. Similarly, change hands to pour for your left nostril.
- ☞ Stand with keeping a shoulder level difference between your feet.
- ☞ Lean a little forward from your trunk and bend the knees a little.
- ☞ Bend the neck to the left side, keeping the ears away from the collars and gaze up.

Practice

- Start to breathe through the mouth and pour the water you have prepared in the *neti* or the pot through your right nostril slowly. The flow of the water should be directed out from the left nostril.

Precautions

- The water should not be hot. Make sure you have taken lukewarm water.
- Do not use too much salt. Mix ½ tps salt in half litre water.
- If you feel the water has gone to the windpipe, then stop immediately and do *kapalabhati*. This rarely happens.
- If you feel recurring pain in the nose or head after the practice, stop practising and consult a yoga expert.

Benefits

- Cleansing of the nasal passage is extremely important to keep the body free of dirt and bacteria.
- The nose has protective vibrating hairs at different levels which do not allow the bacteria and dirt to enter the lungs.
- It draws out excessive heat and thus provides a cooling and soothing effect to the brain.
- Headaches, migraine, sinus cavities, snoring conditions, etc., will be benefitted with this *neti* practice.
- It also has a harmonising effect as it works on the pineal and pituitary glands.
- *Neti* helps remove excess mucous.
- Its practice is also associated with the sensitising and activating of the *Ajna Chakra* in higher spiritual practices.
- *Neti* improves the eye vision and also provides a sparkle to the eyes.

Dhauti (Cleansing)

Dhauti basically means to *cleanse*. There are four types of *Dhauti Kriya* being mentioned in *Gherand Samhita*. They are:

1. *Antara Dhauti* (Internal Cleansing)
2. *Daanth Dhauti* (Teeth Cleansing)
3. *Hrid Dhauti* (Heart Cleansing)
4. *Moola Dhauti* (Rectal Cleansing)

We will be discussing the practice of *Kunjal Kriya* (*Vaman Dhauti*) which is related to *Antara Dhauti* and the *Hrid Dhauti*.

Process

Kunjal Kriya involves drinking of purified lukewarm water mixed with iodised salt, until vomiting sensation appears. Then the water is taken out by inducing vomiting either by drinking more water or through touching the epiglottis.

Technique

- ☞ Drink water mixed with salt (1/2 tbps salt in 1 litre water) till the time that you feel there is no space in the stomach now.
- ☞ Hold water in the stomach for some time.
- ☞ Try to breathe in by filling up the stomach and breathe out by pulling the navel as close to the navel as possible. Repeat this 5 to 10 times after 20 seconds of interval in between.
- ☞ Now stand with the body above the navel bent forward.
- ☞ Water will automatically start coming out now.
- ☞ If it does not happen, then stimulate the epiglottis by touching it with your forefingers so that the water can flow out.
- ☞ Keep taking out until the water taken in the stomach is thrown out.

Precautions

- ☞ Any person suffering from serious ailments should perform it under the guidance of a Yoga expert.
- ☞ Do not haste to throw the water out.
- ☞ If coughing occurs due to any reason, don't panic, just relax for some time.

Benefits

- ☞ The complete alimentary canal gets cleaned.
- ☞ Excess mucous, filthy fermented juices and unnecessary secretions of juices are all removed.
- ☞ Bile, Gastric Juices and Flatulence are also removed.
- ☞ Prevents further accumulation of foreign matter in the system.
- ☞ Forceful vomiting renders the much needed massage to the internal organs.
- ☞ To some extent, it takes off the load from the kidneys, liver and intestines.
- ☞ It also helps to cleanse the cardiac area thus removing the blockage from the centre of heart region in the psychic sense.

Nauli Kriya (Rotation of the Abdominal Rectus Muscles)

The root word, 'Nala' means the 'navel string' that is the *rectus abdominal muscles*. It also means tubular vessel.

Nauli Kriya is the best explained in the said verse, HYP 2:33,34 – "Lean forward, protrude the abdomen and rotate (the muscles) from right to left with speed. This is called *nauli* by the *siddhas*. *Nauli* is the foremost among the *Hatha Yoga* practices. It kindles the digestive fire, removing indigestion, sluggish digestion and all disorders or the *doshas*, bringing about happiness".

The above verse explains the process, techniques and benefits of the practice.

Nauli Kriya is incorporated in three parts.

- *Dakshina Nauli*

  When the rectus abdominal muscles are rotated from left to right, it is called *dakshina nauli.*

- *Vama Nauli*

  When the rectus abdominal muscles are rotated from right to left, it is called *vama nauli.*

- *Madhyama Nauli*

  When the muscles are pulled together and the middle group of muscles protrude, it is called *Madhyama Nauli.*

Technique

- Stand with your legs apart at the shoulder level distance. Bend from the knee a little bit and also bend a bit on the back.
- Press the abdominal muscles inside and then try to push it forward by grouping the muscles in between. Sometimes pressing a bit more firmly on your thighs with your hands helps.
- Now obtain *Uddiyana Bandha* and relax the left side abdominal muscles, while keeping the right side muscles engaged. Sometimes putting more weight in the right side arm and leg helps.
- Now contract the left side muscles while keeping the right side relaxed. Again, putting more weight in the left side arm and leg can help.
- Thus, you need to create a rolling movement to perform the *Nauli Kriya.*

Benefits

- ☞ It improves digestion.
- ☞ It renders a beneficial massage to the entire abdominal organ. The muscles and nerves are stimulated and relaxed simultaneously. The intestine, excretory and urinary organs and the intestine also benefit.
- ☞ Cures the ailments like constipation, indigestion, nervous, diarrhoea, acidity, flatulence, depression, hormonal imbalance, sexual and urinary disorders, diabetes, lack of energy, emotional disturbances.

Basti (Yogic Enema)

It is a *cleansing technique for the colon*, where waste matter from the colon are not completely flushed out by the natural bowel movements. The *Yogic Enema* serves the purpose of its cleansing.

Process

The influx of water in the colon through sitting in a tub where the lower body, only up to the navel is under the water and the sphincter muscles are contracted and expanded.

Technique

- ☞ In the beginning, insert a cathedral (lubricated with non-irritating oil or ghee) approximately 13-15 cms long in the anus.
- ☞ Sit in a tub with navel deep water (Lukewarm).
- ☞ Inhale and practise *Uddiyana Bandha* (compression of the abdominal muscles towards the navel).
- ☞ Now exhale slowly.
- ☞ This should draw in water in the rectal canal.
- ☞ Do not expel the water.

Precautions

- ☞ Do not practise with cold water.
- ☞ Do not practise *Basti* during cold, cloudy and stormy weather.
- ☞ Do not expel water in the tub. Expel it in a toilet as stools may come out with the water.
- ☞ Take rest atleast up to 72 minutes after the practice.

Benefits

- ☞ Appetite increases.
- ☞ Excess *doshas* (body impurities and ailments) are destroyed.

- Body glows as impurities are cleaned.
- Diseases arising from excess wind, bile and mucus are eliminated.

Kapalabhati

Kapalabhati is that which shines the *Kapala* (brain). It is a practice which keeps the region of the nostrils to the lungs of the respiratory tract clean and healthy.

Process

It is done by performing Rapid Exhalation (forceful exhale) and Inhalation (which is a involuntary movement).

Technique

- Sit in *Vajrasana* or *Padmasana*.
- Close your eyes and let the whole system relax. Become aware of your breathing.
- Inhale deeply at first by bulging out the abdominal muscles.
- Forcefully exhale through the nostrils, compressing the abdomen as much as possible. This completes one cycle.
- Inhalation will be an automatic passive function now.
- Again concentrate on forceful exhalation.
- After completing the desired number of cycles, remain with your eyes closed and feel the shining sensation at the forehead, the relaxation and purified effect is experienced in the whole body.
- In the beginning, practise 10 to 15 cycles. You may gradually increase to 60 cycles in a minute and then to 120 cycles in a minute.

Precautions

- While performing *Kapalabhati*, do not lean or bend sideways, forward or backward, as it can cause muscle sprain in the neck or back or may lead to slip disc.
- Keep the facial muscles relaxed, otherwise a muscle catch in the face may occur.
- Do not haste or perform *Kapalabhati* very fast.
- Do not perform this yoga posture if you have High Blood Pressure, Ischemic Heart Disease, Slip Disc, Spondylitis.

Benefits

- Cleanses and purifies the entire system of the body.
- Renders massage to the abdominal organs, thus improving digestion, appetite, etc.

- More oxygen is infused in the lungs and carbon dioxide flushed out.
- Residual air in the lungs is also cleansed during *Kapalabhati*.
- As more oxygen is infused in the cells, lethargy is eliminated and a person gains vigour and vitality.
- Better functioning of the mind, body and brain.
- Persons suffering from obesity, respiratory disorders, digestive problems and diabetes benefit a lot with this practice.

Trataka (Blinkless Gazing)

Trataka involves fixation of gaze at a central point. It may be a body, an eyebrow centre, a nose tip or a candle.

Process

Trataka is a process of concentrating the mind and curbing its oscillating tendencies. It improves concentration and awareness of the inner and outer realms.

Technique

- Sit in *Vajrasana* or *Padmasana* and place your palms on the knee.
- Now stare at the flame of the candle which should be kept at an eye level and at a distance of about 2 feet.
- Be motionless in the practice.
- As tears shed from the eyes, slowly close them and concentrate on the flame visualising it within the body.

Precautions

- Do not lean forward.
- Do not sit in a windy room.
- Do not strain your eye nerves.
- Practise each day and improve. Do not haste.

Benefits

- Strengthens the optic nerves.
- Cures the diseases of the eyes.
- Removes laziness.

Chapter 6

Pranayama

"Bahya abhyantara stambha vrittih desha kala sankhyabhih paridrishtah dirgha sukshmah" 2.50(P.Y.S)

Pranayama has three aspects of external or *outward flow* (exhalation), internal or *inward flow* (inhalation), and the third, which is the absence of both during the transition between them, and is known as *fixedness*, *retention*, or *suspension*. These are regulated by place, time and number, with breath becoming slow and subtle.

'Prana' means 'Breath' and 'control' here means 'channelizing the breath in a harmonious way'.

Thus, *Pranayama* is a practice of *regulation of breath*.

There are three main aspects of Pranayama:

1. Inhalation
2. Exhalation
3. Retention

Things important to know before starting the practice of Pranayama:

- Choose a neat and clean place.
- The room should be well ventilated.
- Use the same place every day for your practice. This intensifies the benefits.
- Do not practise *Pranayama* in an AC room.
- Beginners should not practise in open spaces, e.g. garden, rooftop etc. especially, where temperature is too low or too hot.

Instructions & Precautions while doing Pranayama

- Please do not haste in your practice.
- Do not exert by breathing fast or more than the capacity. Of course, we want to increase the capacity of the Lungs, but do it slowly.

- Listen to your body and mind. Self-discretion is highly advised.
- Learn *Pranayama* only from a learned Guru. Pranayama can eradicate all diseases if it is done properly. If done wrongly, it will aggravate all the diseases and thus may be harmful. *So right practice of Pranayama is a must.*
- Have a light or empty stomach when you practise Pranayama.
- Wait for at least 4-5 hours after meals to start Pranayama.
- Pranayama can be practised before or after taking bath.
- Wear comfortable and loose garments.
- *Padmasana* or *Vajrasana* are best suited for *Pranayama*.
- Keep the body comfortable, stable and relaxed, and the spine, neck and head should be erect.
- Avoid outside disturbance.
- Avoid smoking and/or drinking.
- *Sattvic* food is essential.
- Perform Pranayama with natural breathing.
- Be regular in your practice.

Yogic Breath

Abdominal breath: Movement of the diaphragm is achieved from this technique.

Steps:

- Sit in *Vajrasana* or *Sukhasana* or *Padmasana*.
- One must try to inhale and fill up the abdomen only by expanding the abdominal wall.
- Exhale by contracting the abdominal muscles as much as possible. The navel should move towards the spine as much as possible.
- Relax after sufficient repetition.

Thoracic breath: Movement of the ribs is required in this technique.

Sit in *Vajrasana* or *Sukhasana* or *Padmasana*.

- Inhale and expand the chest. Expansion is especially from the ribs.
- Try not to make any movement of the abdomen. A slight contraction of the abdomen is desired though.
- Exhale and contract the chest downwards and inwards.
- Relax after sufficient repetition.

Shoulder breath: Inflation and deflation of the lungs is achieved from this technique.

- ☞ Sit in *Vajrasana* or *Sukhasana* or *Padmasana.*
- ☞ Cross your arms and place the palms on opposite shoulders.
- ☞ Now inhale by drawing the shoulders and collar bones upwards.
- ☞ Exhale and release the shoulders and collar bones downwards.
- ☞ This movement is similar to the breathing pattern when we stop after running fast and require more breath.
- ☞ Relax after sufficient repetition.

Yogic breathing: Combination of the above three techniques in a continuous flow is known as *Yogic breath.*

- ☞ Sit in *Vajrasana* or *Sukhasana* or *Padmasana.*
- ☞ Inhale and start filling up the abdomen, continue then by expansion of the ribs and then drawing the shoulders upwards. Do not stop at any point. This should be done in one continuous flow.
- ☞ Exhaling, release the shoulders downwards and then contraction of the rib cage and contraction of the abdominal wall take place. This should be done in one continuous flow.
- ☞ Relax after sufficient repetition.

Notes:

- ➤ Repetition can be done a minimum of any round that is comfortable- 1, 2 or 3 rounds.
- ➤ After sufficient practice, 11 rounds will be sufficient.
- ➤ Do not overdo. Continue to the extent where you feel relaxed and are enjoying the practice.
- ➤ Practise *Shavasana* or remain in the sitting pose with eyes closed for some time after the practice of each *Pranayama.*
- ➤ Practise *Shavasana* after the completion of all *Pranayama* practice.

Surya Bhedan (Right Nostril Breathing)

In yogic science, the right nostril is the path to *Surya* (Sun) *Nadi* (Pyschic Passage).

Steps:

- ☞ Sit in *Vajrasana*, *Padmasana* or *Sukhasana,* as comfortable.
- ☞ Fold the right hand at the elbow and close the index finger and the middle finger. The little finger, ring finger and the thumb will remain erect.

- Now close the left nostril with the help of the little finger and the the ring finger. The thumb will remain erect. Let the arm rest close to the armpit.
- Inhale slowly through the right nostril.
- Exhale slowly through the right nostril.
- Follow the pattern of Yogic breath.

Benefits:

- Stimulates the symphathetic nervous system.
- Makes one active.
- Stimulates the left part of the brain.

Rounds:

- 11 rounds is good. Later upon discretion, you may increase.

Chandra Bhedan (Left Nostril Breathing)

In yogic science, the left nostril is the path to *Chandra* (Moon) *Nadi* (Pyschic Passage).

Steps:

- Sit in *Vajrasana*, *Padmasana* or *Sukhasana,* as comfortable.
- Fold the right hand at the elbow and close the index finger and the middle finger. The little finger, ring finger and the thumb should remain erect.
- Now close the right nostril with the help of the thumb. The little finger and the ring finger will remain erect. Let the arm rest close to the armpit.
- Inhale slowly through the left nostril.
- Exhale slowly through the left nostril.
- Follow the pattern of Yogic breath.

Benefits:

- Stimulates the parasympathetic nervous system.
- Specifically, relaxes the mind and body.
- Stimulates the right part of the brain.

Rounds:

- 11 rounds are good. Later upon discretion, you may increase.

Nadi Shodhan (Purification of the Nervous System)

The parasympathetic and the sympathetic nervous system are brought in perfect balance through this practice. The psychic passage – the sun and the moon meet at the *Shushumna Nadi* at the region behind the eyebrow centre. When the flow from both the nostrils is even and together, meditational experience may occur.

Steps:

- ☞ Sit in *Vajrasana*, *Padmasana* or *Sukhasana,* as comfortable.
- ☞ Fold the right hand at the elbow and close the index finger and middle finger. The little finger, ring finger and the thumb will remain erect.
- ☞ Now close the left nostril with the help of the little finger and the ring finger. The thumb will remain erect. Let the arm rest close to the armpit.
- ☞ Inhale slowly through the right nostril.
- ☞ Close the right nostril with the help of the thumb. Exhale slowly through the left nostril releasing the little finger and the ring finger from the left nostril.
- ☞ Now again inhale through the left nostril.
- ☞ Close the left nostril with the help of the little finger and the ring finger. Exhale slowly through the right nostril releasing the thumb from the right nostril.
- ☞ This makes one round of *Nadi Shodhan*.

Benefits:

- ☞ Balances the Sympathetic and the Parasympathetic Nervous System.
- ☞ Gives relief from anxiety, depression, insomnia, fear.
- ☞ Relief from excess gas from the body.
- ☞ Purifies the blood through the removal of toxins.
- ☞ Very effective for stress management.

Rounds:

- ☞ 11 rounds are good. Later upon discretion, you may increase.

Bhramari (Humming Bee Breath)

It is an excellent practice to charge the nerve cells of the brain. The blood circulation towards the brain is enhanced in this practice.

Steps:

- ☞ Sit in *Vajrasana*, *Padmasana* or *Sukhasana* as comfortable.
- ☞ Inhale slowly.
- ☞ Exhaling creates a Humming sound - HMMMMMMMMMMMM MMMMMMM.

Benefits:

- ☞ Removes stress, depression, anxiety and fear.
- ☞ Increases the blood supply to the brain.
- ☞ Awareness is improved at all levels.

Rounds:

- ☞ 11 rounds are good. Later upon discretion, you may increase.

Ujjayi (Diaphragmatic Breath)

'Ujj'- Mind, 'Jayi'- Winning or Victory. This practice eventually helps one to achieve victory over the mind. This is in the sense that, the system becomes relaxed and thoughts are vanished.

Steps:

- ☞ Sit in *Vajrasana*, *Padmasana* or *Sukhasana,* as comfortable.
- ☞ Create suction at the epiglottis, while inhaling through the nostrils.
- ☞ Create vaccum at the epiglottis, while exhaling through the nostrils.
- ☞ This will create a wave sound through the voice chord.

Benefits:

- ☞ Relaxes the mind and helps to explore the subconscious mind.
- ☞ Helpful in insomnia, depression, heart disease.
- ☞ *Ujjayi* reduces the blood pressure.
- ☞ People suffering from serious problems of low blood pressure must take care while practising *Ujjayi*.

Rounds:

- ☞ 11 rounds are good. Later upon discretion, you may increase.

Bhastrika (Bellows Breath)

In this *Pranayama*, one has to try to operate the lungs just as a bellow.

Steps:

- ☞ Inhale and exhale at a very fast pace.
- ☞ After sufficient fast breathing, inhale from the right nostril.
- ☞ Retain the breath.
- ☞ Practise *bandhas*.
- ☞ Exhale through the left nostril.

Benefits:

- ☞ Exchange of oxygen and carbon dioxide is at cell level.
- ☞ Stimulates the heart and the lungs.
- ☞ Improves blood circulation.

Shitali (Cooling Breath)

The purpose of this *Pranayama* is to cool down the Body and the Mind.

Steps:

- Roll the tongue.
- Inhale through the mouth (Passage created by rolling the tongue).
- Release the tongue and take it back inside the mouth and close the mouth.
- Exhale slowly through the nostrils.

Benefits:

- Harmonises the secretion of the Endocrine System.
- Cools the entire body system.
- Lowers High Blood Pressure.
- Relaxes and calms down the Nervous System.

Shitkari (Cools the Body and Quenches the Thirst)

- Cools the system and removes excess heat from the body.

Steps:

- Clinch the upper and the lower teeth together tightly.
- Open your lips.
- Inhale by making a hissing sound.
- Close your lips, release and clinch the teeth and exhale slowly through the nostrils.

Benefits:

- Same as of *Shitali*.

Chapter 7

Bandhas

The Sanskrit word, 'Bandha' means to hold, tighten or lock. The purpose is to lock the *prana* in particular areas and redirect the flow into *Sushumna Nadi.*

There are four Bandhas – Jalandhar, Mool, Uddiyan and Maha Bandha (The combination of the first three).

1. **Jalandhar Bandha (Throat Lock):** Place the palms of the hands on the knees and close your eyes to do this *bandha*. Relaxing your body and inhaling slowly and deeply and retaining breath inside, bend your head forward and press your chin tightly against the chest. Do not inhale or exhale unless the lock has been released and the head is fully upright.
2. **Mool Bandha:** Closing your eyes and sitting in Siddhasana (for men) and *Siddha Yoni Asana* (for women) in a relaxed way, control the perennial/vaginal region. Continue contracting and relaxing the perennial/vaginal region rhythmically, slowly and evenly.
3. **Uddiyana Bandha:**
   - Stand erect with feet half a metre apart.
   - Inhale through your nostrils and bend forward from the waist exhaling all the air through the mouth.
   - Empty your lungs as much as possible.
   - Bend the knee slightly and place the palms of your hands on the thighs, just above the knees. The fingers point downwards. Bend the head forward.
   - Draw the abdomen upward and inward towards the spine. After some time, release the abdominal lock.
4. **Mahabandha:** In this *bandha, Jalandhar Bandha, Uddiyana Bandha* and the Mool Bandha are successively performed and then *Mool Bandha*, Uddiyan a Bandha and the Jalandhar Bandha are released in this order.

Chapter 8

Management of Diseases through Yoga, Pranayama & Yogic Diet

Indtroduction

1. Diabetes

Diabetes is a very common disease nowadays. People of all age groups are a victim of this ailment.

Our blood glucose level should be maintained between 100 to 150 mgs%. This monitoring system consists of two major hormones called the *insulin* and the *glucagon*. The insulin reduces the blood glucose levels and glucagon increases it. Both the insulin and glucagon are produced in the body by a gland known as the pancreas. Its weight is about three to four ounces.

Causes of Diabetes are:

- Heredity
- Overweight
- Dietary faults
- Stress
- Lack of exercise

Yoga Therapy for Diabetes

- *Uddiyana, Agnisara, Nauli* and *Viparit Karani*. These four practices increase the blood flow and are very helpful in curing of this disease.
- *Asanas* useful in diabetes are *Ardhakati Chakrasana, Pada Hastasana, Ardha Chakrasana, Trikonasana, Ardha Matsyendrasana, Mayurasana, Bhujangasana, Dhanurasana* and *Sarvangasana* described in this book.
- *Pranayama, Shavasana* and *Meditation,* all are very useful in this disease.

2. Reducing Weight

Fat surplus of 8% to 15% over the normal weight must be considered as overweight. Beyond that it must be regarded as *obesity*. It is suggested that these people must take their weight every 28 days to keep a watch on their weight.

Causes of Obesity

- Heredity
- Overeating
- Sedentary *Lifestyle*
- Glands and nervous factors
- Watery overweight issue and the electro-chemical balance of the body fluids.

The problem of this weight can be managed by dieting, exercise, rest, breathing, massage and *Yogasanas*. The following *asanas* are recommended:

- *Surya Namaskar*
- *Dhanurasana*
- *Bhujangasana*
- *Halasana*
- *Paschimottanasana*

3. Thyroid

This gland lies in front of the neck, wrapped around the trachea. It is divided into two lobes, one on each side of the neck. Yoga is very useful in treating this disease. Practise *Jalandhar Bandha* for curing this disease.

4. Heart and Circulatory System

The *heart's function* is intimately related to our *emotional metabolism*. Our emotional states directly influence the health of the heart. *Stress* is a very damaging factor in this disease and is known as the prominent cause of a *heart attack*. Medical science says that the degree of cardiac and arterial degeneration is related to the amount of fat and cholesterol consumed in the diet. So proper *yogic diet* is very essential in this case.

Yoga offers the solution of heart diseases in various ways which includes *asanas*, *pranayama* and *yoga nidra*.

5. Respiratory Disorder

This system consist of nose, pharynx, epiglottis, trachea, bronchi and the lungs.

The yogic approach in rectifying imbalances in the respiratory system is very beneficial. *Pranayama* plays a very important role in these cases.

6. Disorder of the Digestive System

The digestive organs, glands and the solar plexus of the nerves are symbolised by our *Manipura Chakra*. The element of fire is related to it. Yogic management for indigestion and constipation include *Pawana Muktasana, Agnisar Kriya, Halasana* and *Fasting*.

Gastric ulcer and *Duodenal ulcer* can be effectively cured by Yogic methods.

7. Joints and Musculo-Skeletal System

Cervical, Spondilitis, Back Pain, Slip Disc and Sciatica are very common nowadays. They can be well attended by *yogic therapy* as well.

8. Urogenital System

This system is governed by the water element. The urinary and reproductive systems are closely interconnected. The urinary tract problems in women, menstrual disorders and other vaginal infections including *leucorrhoea*, disorders of the male reproductive system, sterility, impotence, prostate disease, hernia, hydrocele, etc., can be managed through yogic practices.

9. Insomnia

For a restful sleep and for overcoming insomnia, *yoga is a miracle*. *Sleep is very essential for good health*. Deep sleep or delta sleep is helpful in restoring our health of the body and mind.

Cobra pose, Locust pose, Yoganidra and *Pranayama* are very useful in restful sleep.

Yogic Diet

For Yogic practices, *sattvic food* is very essential.

What is Food?

Food is a mixture of edible substances that are available to us through meal in accordance to particular geographical conditions, environment and seasons.

Functions

A. Biological – Food provides the nutrient to meet our biological requirements – Energy (Carbohydrates), Building Blocks (Proteins), Protection (Fats & Lipids), and Metabolism Regulation (Minerals, Vitamins Anti-Oxidant Providers, etc.).

B. Psychological – Means of Nutrition & Emotional Bonding are essential.

What is Yogic Food: Those type of food substances, which –

1. Facilitate us to keep the most damaging and neuron irritant free radicals, responsible for involuntary oxidative stress, within the threshold limit.
2. Are those, non-irritant, easily digestible, edible substances, which are available for meal in natural form in accordance to the particular geographical conditions, environment and season.

Yogic Food Function

In addition to the aforesaid normal food functions, the Yogic food function which makes difference between the normal foods to Yogic Foods are – **Yogic Food Substances**:

1. Keeps the metabolic rate within the threshold limits, keeps a check on extra free radicals' production.
2. Provides more antioxidants (Super Oxides Dismutase – An Enzyme) to maintain pleasing, soothing and relax the environment of the Body and Mind levels.

Yogic Food and Health

There is a strong connection between our health and what we eat. Recent scientific studies have revealed that the health of a person is governed by the kind of food he eats and that diseases and disabilities can be prevented if he consumes the right kind of food in the right time and in the right proportion. In the 21st century, there would be more of Dieticians in comparison to the doctors who treat the diseases. The responsibilities of the governments would be to mainly provide the right kind of information/ facilities that would ensure providing food with the right nutritional composition, unpolluted air, water and NATURAL FOOD, RATHER YOGIC FOOD, etc. The public need to be sensitised and empowered with knowledge pertained to the vital link between the Yogic food and health.

Traditional societies in the world over have selected and perfected their food from the local resources after hundreds of years of trial, error or empirical selection and more particularly, the clinical experiment they did. In fact, there are different kinds of foods consumed in different season particularly India, China and other Asian countries that provide valuable information on this matter. In India, there was a strong tradition of different dietary regimes in different seasons in different agro-climatic regions. The Indian traditional systems of medicines, particularly the Ayurveda also gives a detailed account on the type of food to be taken by the people in different seasons and in different geoclimatic conditions. It has also recommended various do's and don'ts in the selection and combination of food articles.

For example the Ayurveda masters recommended consumption of vegetables like bottle, gourd, lady finger, snake gourd, spinach and red pumpkin in winter season (Dec-Jan) and avoid sunflower, drumstick, gourd, brinjal, etc., in this very season.

The vegetables and fruits, the health protective, disease preventive and health promotive components of food (Anti-Oxidant Nutrients Provider) contribute to the requirement of essential minerals, vitamins, poly-phenols and other Phyto-Chemicals that enable us to adjust and adapt in different agroclimatic conditions and seasons as well as for people of different constitutions and age groups. The fruits and vegetables of tropical region have powerful anti-oxidant and other elements that help in protecting us from harmful radiations, combating superoxide radicals and providing better immunity from many diseases. There are innumerable examples that can be cited on the food articles consumed by people in different parts of the world.

It is the understanding of health protective component of the traditional food and other food regimes of India and Asian countries that a new range of HEALTHY YOGIC FOOD, functional food and neutraceuticals are emerging and becoming popular in the world. Indeed, we are entering a new paradigm shift in our approach to health and medicine. While we are discarding many of our traditional foods, many western countries are busy in studying and adapting the *traditional Yogic Diet* adopted by our ancestors. It is high time that we take a fresh look over our traditional foods and dietary habits from the point of modern scientific knowledge and understanding and revive the use of the traditional food articles and dietary patterns to promote and protect the health of people. The western world after realising the folly of the fast food and culture, are now turning to the ETHNIC YOGIC FOOD of the Third World countries.

Yogic Foods deal with Oxidative Stress. *Yogic food* plays a very important role in managing stress, especially, Oxidative STRESS – it may cause – Cancer, Auto-immune disease by gene mutation, Diabetes, Arthritis, Osteoporosis Libido, Hypertension even Psychiatric disorders, if goes beyond the Thresh-Hold Limits.

By virtue of wisdom, since the ancient times, visionary people visualised that human beings shall be compelled to face stress, unknowingly, of course willingly too. The body is capable of maintaining the internal environment within very narrow range called the *Thresh-Hold Limits.*

For example, in Hindu Mythology – Frame a unique 9 day systematic religious fasting system bi-yearly during *Navratri* (In April and October) along with the different modes of worship.

For fasting period, the visionary people have laid down guidelines for the meal pattern and food item restrictions, besides linking them with religious *Astha*. So, community in mass can fallow that and remain healthy, and manpower can contribute at the optimum level in development.

In April and October, the season in under window period of change from winter to summer, and summer to winter. The Human body is in the process of making adjustment according to change in the outer environment, so many chemical reactions are going on. As result, heavy amounts of free radicals are being produced and body's self-mechanism is busy to deal with these free radicals to keep the oxidative stress with Threshold limits.

So, any kind of extra demand made on body may produce more free radical taking oxidative stress beyond threshold limit. This may lead to any permanent damage or chronic aliments or acute ailments may convert in to the chronic one. So, they prescribed meal patterns and food items during, fasting period.

Yogic Food Substances & Properties

Fruits provide the simplest form of glucose (fructose – ready energy). Some fruits besides *Guava, Papaya,* etc. should be included in *Yogic Diet*. Details of some fruits are as follows:

Apple: Protects the heart, prevents constipation, blocks diarrhoea, improves lung capacity and cushions joints.

Banana: Protects the heart, lessens cough, strengthens bones, controls blood pressure, blocks diarrhoea.

Beans: Prevents constipation, helps hemorrhoid, lowers cholesterol, combats cancer, stabilises blood sugar.

Beets: Controls BP, combats cancer, strengthens bones, protects the heart, aids weight loss.

Blueberries: Combats cancer, protects the heart, stabilises blood sugar, boosts memory, and prevents constipation.

Cabbage: Combats cancer, prevents constipation, promotes weight loss, protects the heart, helps hemorrhoids.

Carrots: Saves eyesight, protects the heart, prevents constipation, combats cancer, promotes hunger.

Cantaloupe: Saves eyesight, controls Blood Pressure, lowers cholesterol, combats cancer, supports immune system, etc.

Vitamins, Minerals (as anti-oxidants, roughs – good for cleaning GIT & help in clearing bowels and potassium for lowering stress at cellular level.

Dry Fruits provides essential oils, minerals, vitamins required in traces, for skin and visceral muscles toning, Vegetable are calories-free food items which provides plenty of water, vitamins, minerals. Spices, Cloves (Syzygium Aromaticum) – provides oral hygiene, prevention from cold and cough and Cardamom (Elettaria cardamomu) – checks the acidity problem, helps in digestion, and works as a mouth-freshener.

Rock Salt provides high Potassium and low Sodium – it releases the internal fluid stress on cell membranes and lowers the chances on untamed death of cell from rapture. It helps to the functioning of Sodium - Potassium Pump at the cell membrane.

Geminated Food substances are balanced diets, provides easily digestible macro-nutrients and extra amount of anti-oxidants – minerals and vitamins.

Obstacles: In today's world, the very scientific concept of Yogic Food formula to keep a healthy life, taken either as fashion or mistaken or wrongly taken – people taking more heavy or taking no food, both or not aware about the biological base of concept.

Conclusion: Inclusion of Yogic Food substances in regular meals shall provide space to our body systems to rearrange the physiological activities to you. Away from so many ailments at the same time, it provides you a healthy life and economy.

Suggestion: Due to hectic life schedules, environmental imbalance, irrational use of medicines, the level of Oxidative Stress is much higher in human body. So, *Yogic Food must be recommended on the top priority.*

Chapter 9

Yoga for Seniors

Yoga is very appropriate for old persons and seniors. In modern times, they suffer from a lot of problems. The benefits of Yoga are very helpful to them in their old age. They need help through yoga in the following spheres:

Flexibility

Yoga can improve the flexibility of their bodies. It can improve the quality of life, strengthening their bodies, improving the balance and flexibility of the bodies.

Improved Circulation

Yoga improves the flow of blood and strengthens the heart, lungs and almost all the vital organs of the body. It makes the body to stay healthy and fight diseases.

Better Alignment

Yoga can be very helpful in body alignment. It makes our postures balanced and solves many back, neck and joint muscle problems of the old age. This alignment helps to correct the postural imbalances in the old age.

Decrease Insomnia

In old age, people generally suffer from *insomnia*. Yoga can heal this major problem of old age. It calms the nervous system and helps relaxation.

- Benefits of yoga are both physical and non-physical.
- It increases the body awareness which is very helpful in avoiding injuries in old age.
- Breathing, relaxation and meditation help reducing the effects of stress in old age.
- Yoga is also very useful for spiritual advancement and positive outlook in life of old persons.

Precautions

In old age, the physical body of our or the old people seniors is becomes very fragile. So old persons should always consult doctors before trying to practise Yoga, especially if they suffer from any chronic conditions or ailments.

Yoga has been also very useful to alleviate arthritis pain, bone density and osteoporosis. It is very helpful in chronic pains. It may help in dementia and help them to maintain their mental and intellectual equilibrium.

Recommended Asanas

- Sukhasana
- Siddhasana
- Makarasana
- Shavasana

Recommended Pranayama Practices

- Yogic breathing
- Nadi Shodhan
- Bhramari
- Kapalabhati

The details of these *asanas* and *pranayamas* have been discussed in this book.

Laughter Yoga – The Best Medicine for Seniors

Laughter Yoga is the best medicine for seniors to keep them *healthy and happy*. They can get rid of stress, worry and depression. It also helps their emotional and mental balance and is very helpful in loneliness and isolation. It also generates their positive thoughts and reduces the negativity in them. It is very helpful also in their physical illness as wellness. It cures their depression, improves their communication and relations.

Meditation

Seniors must do meditation. It is better to practise 20 minutes of mindfulness each day along with deep breathing. As we age, our focus shifts. We start to worry about death, illness and finances. We live in stress and anxiety. So constant practise of meditation can help us lot.

Chapter 10

Yoga for Women

Yoga for women is now becoming more and more popular. In foreign countries also, women are learning yoga in a very enthusiastic way. They are more Health conscious and they think that Yoga is a very effective way of making them healthy and fit. Women have many common diseases in modern times. Some of them are:

1. *Amenorrhea* : Absence of menstruation
2. *Dysmenorrhea*: Painful menstruation
3. *Uterine hemorrhage*, Tumours, Fibroids and Ovarian cysts.

Menstruation starts at the age of about 12 years and ends between 45–55 years. *Menopause* is also a very sensitive stage in a women's life. It leads to major changes such as hormonal, physical and psychological. *Yoga is very useful in dealing with such problems.* The type of yoga recommended for women are: B*hakti Yoga, Bahirang yoga, Karma yoga, Mantra yoga, Hath yoga, Jnana yoga, Kundalini yoga, Surya yoga*. They can choose any these yogas suitable to them. There are some yoga experts who say that stiff type of yoga is not suitable for women. It may change their body chemistry but yoga cannot be forbidden for women. Yoga is essential for women at every stage of her life. It is also very interesting to note that Lord Shiva, the great yogi, has first initiated his consort Parvati in yoga. Other women of ancient India like Maitrey, Gargi, Tara and other Yoginis practised yoga. *Yoga does not believe in sex discrimination*. So in spite of many bodily disadvantages in case of women, yoga cannot and should not be denied to them. Disadvantages of a female body include: (1) relatively smaller lung capacity, (2) Pregnancy, (3) motherhood, (4) tenderness, (5) Prejudice against hard work, etc. It has also been noted that in women the liver, stomach, spleen, kidneys, pancreas and colons are relatively larger than men. *Asanas* recommended for women are *Padmasana, Parvatasana, Konasana, Garudasana, Hastapadasana, Matsyasana, Viprit karni, Bhujangasana, Halasana, Makarasana, Shashank asana* and *Shavasana*. These *asanas* has been described already in this book.

Yoga is important for a women in four important stages of her life:

1. Family Planning

2. Pregnancy
3. Menstruation
4. Menopause

Following are the description:

1. **Family Planning:** The remedy sought through pills and loops is not very useful. So, yoga, meditation and purity in sex life must also be practised. Yoga also recommends *Vajroli* (Thunderbolt) and Sahajoli (Spontaneous) *mudras* for men and women respectively.
2. **Pregnancy:** During pregnancy, many simple and easy *asanas* can be done except those that put pressure on the abdomen. No *Uddiyana Bandha* should be done during pregnancy. We should pay our attention to the health of legs and *apana vayu of women* during pregnancy because *apana vayu* is the wind that holds the child in the womb. Moreover, no inversions should be practised after the fifth month. *Asanas* should be a voided during pregnancy are *Paschimottanasana, Trikonasana, Baddha Padmasana, Chakorasana, Gandabherundasana*, etc.
3. **Menstruation:** Menstruation begins at about 12 years and ends at about 55 years. A number of diseases are connected with menstruation. They respond well when treated with *Yogasana. Recommended asanas are Konasana, Padmasana, Swastikasana and Yog a Nidra*. It is recommended that one or two days before the cycle starts, all *asanas* which put pressure on the abdomen should be stopped. Once the red bleeding stops on the 4th or 5th day, a mild practice of *yogasanas* can be done.
4. **Menopause:** After the age of 50, *Vata* increases in both men and women. So paying close attention to the rhythm of breath is necessary. In this age, both the cysts and fibroids come about due to stress, diet and lifestyle. Yogasanas can help a lot. The *asanas* practised at this age are *Ardha Baddha Pamasana, Paschimottanasana, Konasana and Supta Padmasana*.

In a nut-shell, I am prescribing certain yogas which should be practised by women. Their description is given in the next pages.

Recommended Yogas:

☞ *Tadasana*, Thigh exercise
☞ *Dhanurasana, Bhujangasana*
☞ *Gomukhasana, Anulom Vilom*
☞ *Mandukasana, Shalabhasana*

Tadasana & Thigh Exercise

Dhanurasana & Bhujangasana

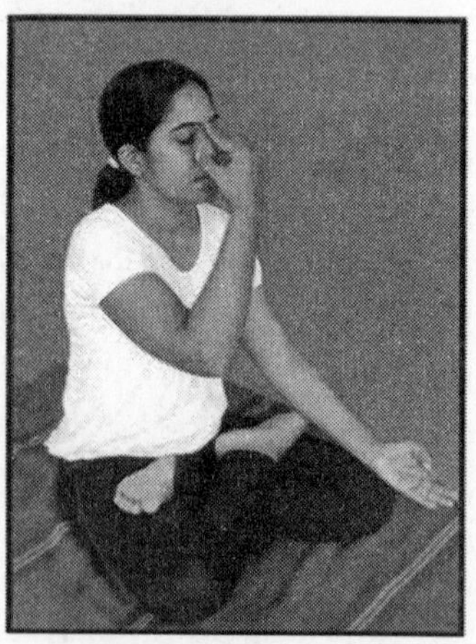

Gomukhasana & Anulom Vilom

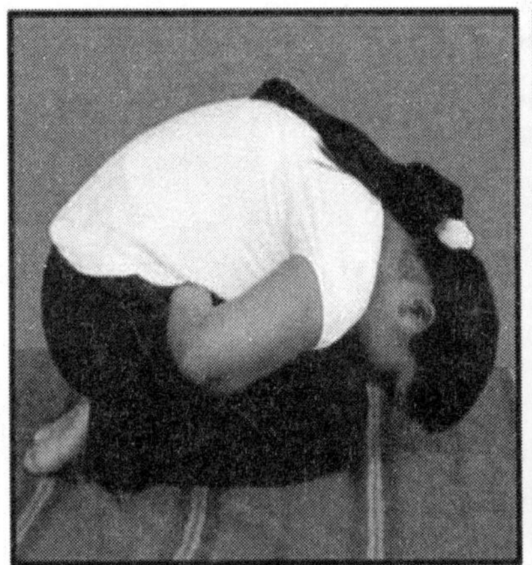
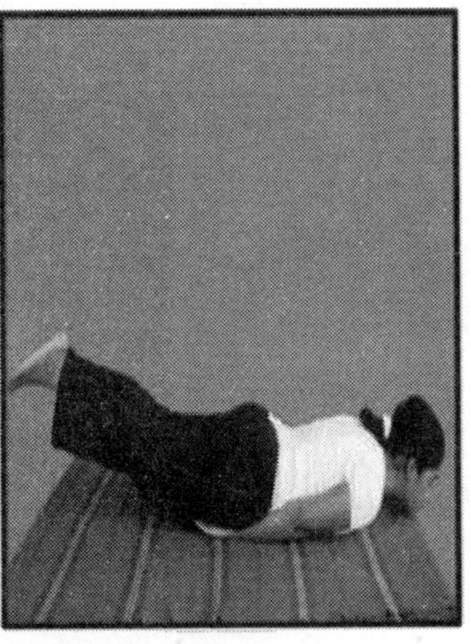

Mandukasana & Shalabhasana

Chapter 11

Yoga for Children & Students

Yoga is the greatest power. By gradual yogic practices, the body and the mind, both become strong and balanced. The practice of *yogasanas* make the body strong and elastic. *Pranayama, the breath control is very beneficial for mind control*. Through the practice of yoga, one is able to know, observe and control the body and mind. Children and students both need to learn yoga. There are certain qualifications which all our children and students need to learn Yoga. These are: Body Purification, Lightness of Body, Strength of the Mind and Concentration Ability, Patience and Steadfastness.

For purification of the body, students should be taught *Neti, Basti, Tratak, Kapalabhati* and other *Pranayamas* like *Nadisodhan, Surya Bhedan, Ujjayi, Sheetali, Bhastrika* and *Bhramri.*

Pranvayu (Oxygenated fresh air) should be retained inside the body as long as possible. It should come out of the body as little as possible. This is the secret of life, energy and power. Retention of breath produces power. This retention of breath is call *kumbhak*. The practice should be learnt from the very beginning in life.

Yogic Asanas: In ancient times, boys were taught yoga between the age of 8–10 years. In this age, the pineal gland of the boys is very active and it starts decreasing afterwards and in the old age, it becomes very short. This gland controls the activities of the mind. So, yoga should be learn from the early age, between 8–10 years. The next gland that controls our mind is known as *pituitary gland* which starts activating at this age. So, for emotional and mental balance, activation of both these glands lead to a balance of energy in students. The following *Asanas* and *Pranayama* are recommended for boys and students:

Pranayama: *Nadi Sodhan Pranayama, Gayatri Mantra, Relaxation Techniques, Bhramari Pranayama, Trataka*, etc.

Asanas: *Surya Namaskar, Sukhasana, Vajrasana, Padamasana, Gomukhasana* (Cow head pose), *Simhasana* (The Lion pose), *Parvatasana, Halasana, Paschimottanasana, Trikonasana,* Anterior Stretching *asanas* such as *Bhujangasana, Matsyasana* (Fish Pose), *Chakrasana* and *Shalabhasana*.

Chapter 12

Yoga for Managing Stress

Concept of Stress

Stress is an everyday unavoidable experience of life. ***Dr. Hars Sevel***, expert of *stress management,* tells us: "Stress is the wear and tear on your body caused by life's events." It is the sum total of body's physical, mental and chemical reactions to circumstances which cause fear, irritation, worry, anxiety and excitement. Stress is purely subjective. It is basically a state of mind in response to a situation.

Effect of Stress

Due to physical and mental reaction, stress deeply affects our body and mind causing many acute and chronic diseases. The symptoms of these ailments can be seen clearly.

Physical Symptoms

Headache, High Blood Pressure, Obesity, Overweight, Loss of Appetite, Constipation, Diarrhoea, Acidity, Peptic Ulcer, Insomnia, Fatigue, Muscular Strain, Back Ache, Asthma, Ahoking of Throat and emotional problems, sexual problems, menstrual distress, Arthritis, etc.

Mental Symptoms

Feeling of nervousness, anxiety, depression, irritation while communication with family members and fellow colleagues at work, worry due to poor financial position, unnecessary fear of getting incurable diseases like cancer, diabetes, etc., and fear of death of someone close, loss of zeal to live, suicidal tendency, incapability of laughing loud and leading happy life, superiority and inferiority feeling so always feel insulted and neglected, feeling of pain of loneliness and unable to share their problems with others, lack of concentration and develop habit of taking alcohol and toxic drugs to avoid facing problems, etc.

Sources of Stress

There can be four sources of stress. Lack of adjustment with environment, e.g. weather and season, noise, traffic and pollution, etc.

Social pressure like financial problems, unemployment, fear of facing interviews, disagreement with co-workers, accident or death of near and dearones, etc.

Psychological – Feeling adult from childhood, menopause, sickness, aging effect, malnutrition, insomnia, lack of physical labour and exercises, guilty consciousness, inferiority or superiority complex, ego, anxiety for past events and worry for the future problems.

Thought – Excitement in thoughts due to negativity caused by reactions to external events and circumstances.

How to Manage Stress

- Change in dietary pattern – more nutrition, stress relieving food should be taken.
- Subtle exercises, Asanas and Pranayama mentioned in this book.
- Proper meditation of flame, ocean, colours, light, etc.
- Music therapy & *mantra chikitsa*
- Avoid isolation and become part of society and devote time for social service.
- Learn being, becoming, relating, thinking, i.e. *The art of living*.
- Proper Relaxation in *Yog Nidra*.

Note: Mental health is the sum total of emotional stability, maturity of character, ability to cope with stresses of life, ability to judge reality accurately, ability to evaluate things with foresight, ability to love and to sustain affectionate relationship with people around you.

Core of the management of Stress is Stimulation-Relaxation Combine

When the mind gets to a state of lethargy, stimulate and awaken it; as it starts speeding up and distraction sets in to calm it down again.

It is evident from the above that *neither depression nor tension* is helpful for the body. Every activity involves stress and is undesirable in the life. But as excess of everything is bad and harmful, neither we can go for depression nor tension or overactivity.

Steps for Relieving the Excessive Stress

1. Sitting

a. Sit with stretched legs, hands up, breath out and touch the toe, go up.

b. Sit in *Vajrasana* and lie down in *Sasankasana* and *Yoga Mudra*.

2. Breathing Exercises

a. Sit in *Sukhasana*, *Siddhasana* or any other sitting pose.

b. Basrika – Long and deep breathing in Chest.

c. *Anulom Vilom* – Alternate Breathing – Total breathing from navel to nostrils.

d. Kapaal Bhaati – Concentrate only on exhaling.

e. Vahya Vritti – Exhale and hold out your breaths.

f. Abhyantar Vritti – Inhale and hold in your breaths.

3. Relaxation

Lie down on your back and in a relaxed position. Think that every part of your body is relaxed and free from any disease or tension in the following sequence (Right leg, the 1st toe, 3rd toe, 5th toe, sole, heel, ankle, calf muscle, thigh muscle, waist, armpit and shoulder, then similarly, start the same procedure from the 1st toe of the left leg up to left shoulder, then right arm, thumb, index finger, middle finger, ring finger, little finger, palm, wrist, forearm, elbow and upper arm, then repeat the procedure from the left hand upto the left upper arm, then head, upper part, right and left temples, forehead, right brow and left brow, right eye and left eye, right ear and left ear, right cheek and left cheek, nose, upper and lower lips and jaws, tongue and chin, then neck front and back, chest (right and left), heart, lungs, liver, spleen, stomach, intestines (large and small), kidneys, pancreas, genital and excretory organs and spine from neck to bottom. While visualising parts of the body, mentally repeat its name and feel that it is relaxed and healthy.

There is another powerful yogic relaxation technique known as *Yoga Nidra* described below.

4. Yoga Nidra

a. Lie down on the back. Keep your hands 6 inches apart from the body, palms facing upward, legs 6 inches apart, head in a comfortable position.

b. Affirm mentally that you will remain awakened throughout the process.

c. Go on hearing the inner voice and mentally follow. Do not interpret or judge. It is alright whether you understand the instructions or do not.

d. Close your eyes and remain awaked inside.

e. *You are a peaceful and enlightened soul, free from any disease or stress.* You have been given the body which is separate.

f. Visualise that your soul goes out of your body into the infinite universe.

g. See that your body is lying flat on the ground. It is made of 5 elements and each element in the universe purifies itself in your body.

h. Visualise that your body is lighter going up and up 2 feet, 100 feet and in the outer *akash* purifies the inner *akash* of the body. *The Outer air purifies the Inner air in the body*. About 80% is water in your body and so is in the universe. It is raining and your body is coming down with the rains. You are taking a refreshing shower under the stream running down the mountain. You are floating with the current of the river visualising the banks on both the sides. Forests, villages, folks and animals, wild animals, city, temple, fair, etc. Go on floating effortlessly. *Do not catch hold of anything that creates bondage.* A river flows towards the sea in the same way, your soul goes to the *super soul*. You have reached the ocean. You see the blue sky and the blue ocean. Your body is floating on the sea waves. Enjoy going up and down, up and down, up and down.

i. Your body has come on the shore covered with mud. The Earth is purifying your earth inside the body.

j. Dig it up and place the body on the fire and enjoy that your feet are burning, hands are burning, your whole body is burning. The fire is extinguished. You have got the pure and healthy body. Enter into it now.

k. Visualise this and stand up and start walking towards the garden. You see beautiful flowers, butterflies, etc. Hear the chirping of birds, and enjoy the cold breeze of the nature. Move on and enter into the jade dark tunnel in front of you. Do not be afraid. Light is at the other end. You are out of the tunnel. See there is a pond and a lotus leaf, a small baby is on the leaf enjoying. You see the baby and then move in another tunnel darker than the first. Now, slowly come out. There is a temple and a saint is sitting and meditating in front of it. *Yajna* is being performed. You sit for a while and meditate. Move out in the third darkest and biggest tunnel which take you to the road full of rush. Cars, buses, scooters are running. On the side parks, young players are playing. Go on the side of the road. You see that some persons are going with a body on their shoulders. They keep the body in a wooden altar and fire is lit. Only ashes remain. This is the story of your body too! Child, young, adolescent, old, dead and ashes. *But You are a Soul who never dies.* Try to merge your Soul in the Supreme self. Feel *Anand, Anand, Anand* of the Supreme.

l. Take three deep breaths. Feel the touch of the ground and the body. Hear the different sounds and smell. Slowly get up at your leisure.

Chapter 13

Therapeutic Index

Acidity

- **Asana**: *Vajrasana* for 10 minutes after every meal.
- **Pranayama**: *Nadi Shodhan, Bhramari.*
- **Shatakarma**: *Agnisar Kriya, Kunjal.*
- **Other**: *Yoga nidra.*

Anaemia

- **Asana**: *Surya Namaskara, Bhjangasana, Sarvangasana, Halsana, Matsyasana* and *Paschimottasana.*
- **Pranayama**: *Nadi Shodhan, Sheetali, Seetkari, Ujjayi and Shavasana.*

Angina Pectoris

- **Asana**: *Pawanamuktasana, Makarasana, Hasta Utthanasana*
- **Pranayama**: *Ujjayi, Nadi Shodhan, Bhramari* (no retention of breath).
- **Other**: *Yoga Nidra.*

Arthritis

Joint pain also known as *arthralgia* is defined as pain stiffness or swelling in or around a joint. *Inflammatory joint pain is termed as arthritis*. There are **360 joints** in the **human body**. There are various kinds of joints such as ball and socket joints, the condyloid joints, the hinge joints, the pivot joints, the gliding jopints in the ankles, wrists and the spine, etc.

Yoga can be very helpful in healing of diseases. The **six** *asanas* useful are:

- **Asana**: Supta Padangushtasana (leg raise), *Dwipada Supta Pawanamuktasana* (Lying leg hug), *Ardha Salabbhasana* (Half locust, advanced), *Parvatasana, Trikonasana.*

- ☞ **Pranayama**: *Nadi Shodhan, Abdominal Breathing, Bhramari, Kapalabhati.*
- ☞ **Shatakarma**: *Neti, Kunjal.*
- ☞ **Other**: *Yoga Nidra* and *Meditation.*

Asthma

- ☞ **Asana**: *Surya Namaskar, Shashankasana, Sarvangasana, Supta Vajrasana, Matsyasana* and Backward bending asanas including *Shavasana* with breath awareness.
- ☞ **Pranayama**: *Nadi Shodhan, Bhastrika, Kapalabhat*i and Deep Abdominal Breathing.
- ☞ **Shatkarma**: *Jal Neti* and *Kunjal.*

Back Ache

- ☞ **Asana**: P*awanamuktasana, Supta Vajrasana, Marjari-asana, Shashankasna Bhujangasana, Tadasana, Kati Chakrasana and Makrasana.*
- ☞ **Pranayama**: *Ujjayi, Bhramari.*

Blood Pressure

- ☞ **Asana**: *Pawanamuktasana, Siddhasana*, all relaxation poses.
- ☞ **Pranayama**: *Nadi Shodhan, Sheetali, Sheetkari, Ujjayi* and *Bhramari.*

Blood Pressure (Low)

- ☞ **Asana**: *Surya Namaskar.*
- ☞ **Pranayama**: *Bhstrika, Kapalabhati* and *Surya Bheda.*
- ☞ **Mudra**: *Vipreeta Karni.*
- ☞ **Bandha**: All *bandhas.*

Cancer

- ☞ **Asana**: *Pawanamuktasana, Surya Namaskar.*
- ☞ **Pranayama**: *Nadi Shodhan, Bhramari, Ujjayi.*
- ☞ **Shatkarma**: *Tratak.*
- ☞ **Other**: *Amaroli, Yoga Nidra* and *Meditations.*

Constipation

- ☞ **Asana**: *Tadasana, Kati Chakrasana, Surya Namaskar, Pawanamuktasana, Vajrasana, Trikonasana* and *Matsyasana* including spinal twist *asanas* like *Halasana.*
- ☞ **Pranayama**: *Nadi Shodhan.*
- ☞ **Mudra**: *Ashwani.*

Depression

- ☞ **Asana**: *Surya Namaskar* and all backward bending, standing and twisting *asanas*.
- ☞ **Pranayama**: *Bhastrika, Kapalabhati*, Abdominal Breathing.
- ☞ **Shatakarma**: *Neti, Kunjal.*

Diabetes

- ☞ **Asana**: *Surya Namaskar, Tadasana, Shashankasana, Supta Vajrasana, Paschimottasana, Bhujangasana, Halasana, Sarvangasana, Matsyasana* and *Shavasana.*
- ☞ **Pranayama**: *Nadi Shodhan, Bhramari, Ujjayi* and *Bhastrika.*

Diarrhoea and Dysentery

- ☞ **Asana**: *Pawanamuktasana, Vajrasana, Surya Namaskar.*
- ☞ **Pranayama**: *Nadi Shodhan, Bhramari, Sheetali, Sheetkari.*
- ☞ **Shatkarma**: *Laghoo Shankhprakshalana.*

Gout

- ☞ **Asana**: *Pawanamuktasana.*

Impotence

- ☞ **Asana**: *Pawanamuktasana, Surya Namaskar, Sarvangasana* and *Halasana.*
- ☞ **Pranayama**: *Nadi Shodhan, Bhastrika, Ujjayi.*
- ☞ **Bandha**: *Moolbandha.*
- ☞ **Mudra**: *Vajroli, Ashwini.*

Insomnia

- ☞ **Asana**: *Pawanamuktasana, Shashankasana, Shavasana.*
- ☞ **Pranayama**: *Bhramari, Ujjayi.*
- ☞ **Shatakarma**: *Trataka.*

Kidney

- ☞ **Asana**: *Surya Namaskar, Supta Vajrasana, Shashankasana, Bhujangasana, Trikonasana, Matsyasana* and all backward bending *asanas*.
- ☞ **Pranayama**: *Bhastrika.*
- ☞ **Bhandha**: *Uddiyana.*

Liver

- ☞ **Asana** : *Paschimottasana, Vakrasana, Matsyendrasana.*
- ☞ **Shatakarma**: *Kunjal*

Menstruation

- ☞ **Asana**: *Surya Namaskar, Pawanamuktasana, Bhujangasana, Shalabhasana, Dhanurasana, Paschimottanasana, Halasana.*
- ☞ **Pranayama**: Abdominal breathing, *Nadi Shodhan, Ujjayi, Bhramari.*
- ☞ **Mudras**: *Ashwini, Vipreeta Karani, Vajroli.*
- ☞ **Bandhas**: All *Bandhas.*

Obesity

- ☞ **Asana**: *Pawanamuktasana, Vajrasana, Surya Namaskar, Halasana, Vipreeta Karani* and *Matsyasana.*
- ☞ **Pranayama**: *Bhastrika, Sheetali* and *Sheetkari.*

Prostate Gland

- ☞ **Asana**: *Pawanamuktasana, Vajrasana* and *Siddhasana.*
- ☞ **Mudra**: *Vajroli Mudra.*
- ☞ **Bandha**: *Mool Bandha.*

Thyroid and Parathyroid

- ☞ **Asana**: *Surya Namaskar, Pawanamuktasana, Sarvangasana, Halasana, Matsyasana* and all backward bending *asanas*.
- ☞ **Pranayama**: All *pranayamas.*
- ☞ **Mudra**: *Vipreet Karani Mudra.*
- ☞ **Bandha**: *Jalandhara Bandha.*
- ☞ **Shatakarma**: *Neti.*

Ulcer (Peptic and Duodenal)

- ☞ **Asana**: *Pawanamuktasana, Vajrasana* and all relaxation postures.
- ☞ **Pranayama**: *Nadi Shodhan, Ujjayi, Sheetali* and *Sheetkari.*

Chapter 14

Appendix – Yoga Aphorisms

Yogashchittvrittinirodha: Yoga is restraining the mind-stuff (chitta) from taking various forms (Vrittis).

Tada Drashtruh Swarupevasthanam: At that time of the concentration the seer (purusha) rests in his own (unmodified) state.

Vrittisarupyamitratra: At other times (other than that of concentration) the seer is identified with the modifications.

Vratyah Panchashtayah Klishtaklishtah: There are five clases of modifications, (some) painful and (others) not painful.

Praman-Viparyaya-Vikalp-Nidra-Smritayah: (These are) right knowledge, indiscrimination, verbal delusion,sleep and memory.

Pratyakshanumagamah Pramanani: Direct perception, inference and competent evidence are proofs.

Viparyayomithyagyanamatdrupapratishtham: Indiscrimination is false knowledge not established in real nature.

Shabdgyananupati Vastushunyo Vikalpah: Verbal delusion follows from words having no (corresponding) reality.

Abhav-Pratyayalambna Vritirnidra: Sleep is the vritti which embraces the feeling of voidness.

Anubhutvishyasampramoshah Smriti: Memory is when the (vrittis of) perceived subjects do not slip away (and through impressions come back to consciousness).

Abhyasvairagyabhyam Tannirodha: Their control is by practice and non-attachment.

Tatra Sthitau Yatnobhyasah: Continuous struggle to keep them (the Vrittis) perfectly restrained is practice.

Satudirghkalnairantaryasatkarasevitodridhbhumih: It becomes firmly grounded by long constant efforts with great love (for the end to be attained).

Drishtanushravikavishyavitrishnasya vashikarsangya vairagyam: That effect which comes to those have given up their thirst after objects, either seen or heard, and which wills to control the objects, non-attachments.

Tatparam purushrupatergunvatrishnyam: That is extreme non-attachment which gives up even the qualities, and comes from the knowledge of (the real nature of) the purusha.

Vitarkvicharanandasmiritanugamat sampragyatah: The concentration called right knowledge is that which is followed by reasoning, discrimination, bliss, unqualified egoism.

Virampratyayabhyaspurvah Sanskarasheshonyah: There is another Samadhi which is attained by the constant practice of cessation of all mental activity, which the Chitta retains only the unmanifested impressions.

Bhav-Pratyayo Videh-Prakritilyanam: (this Samadhi when not followed by extreme non-attachment) becomes the cause of the re-manifestation of the Gods and of those who become merged in the nature.

Shraddha-Virya-Smriti-Samadhi-Pragya-Poorvak Itresham: To others (this Samadhi) comes through faith, energy, memory, concentration, and discrimination of the real.

Tivrasamveganamasannah: Success is speedy for the extremely energetic.

Mridumadhyadhimatritvattatopi Visheshah: The success of Yogis differs according as the means they adopt are mild, medium or intense.

Ishvarpranidhanadva: Or by devotion to Ishvara.

Kleshkarmvipakshaiyairparamrishtah Purushvishesh Ishvarah: Ishvara (the Supreme Ruler) is the special Purusha, untouched by misery, actions, their results, and desires.

Tatra Niratishayam Sarvagyatvabijam: In Him becomes infinite that all-knowingness which in others is (only) a germ.

Sapoorveshamapi Guruh Kalenanvachchhedat: He is the Teacher of even the ancient teachers, being not limited by time.

Tasya Vachakah Pranavah: His manifesting word is AUM.

Tajjpastadarthbhavanam: The repetition of this (AUM) and meditating upon its meaning(is the way).

Tatah pratyakchetnadhigmopyantarayabhavshracha: From that is gained (the knowledge of) introspection, and the destruction of obstacles.

Vyadhi-Styan-Sanshaya-Pramadalasyavirati-Bhrantidarshanalabdh

bhumikatvanavsthitatvani Chittvkshepastentarayah: Disease, mental laziness, doubt, lack of enthusiasm, lithargy, clinging to sense enjoyments, false perceptions, non-attaining concentration, and falling away from the state when obtained, are the obstructing distractions.

Dukhah Daurmanasyaangmejayatva-Shravasprashravasa Vikshep-sahbhuvah: Greif, mental distress, tremor of the body, irregular breathing accompany non-retention of concentration.

Tatpratishedharthmekatatvabhyasah: To remedy this, the practice of one subject (should be made).

Maitri-karunamuditopekshanam Sukhadukhapunyapunyavishayanam Bhavnatishrichattprasadanam: Friendship, mercy, gladness, and indifference, being thought of in regard to subjects happy, unhappy, good, and evil respectively, pacify the *chitta.*

Prachchhardan-Vidharnabhyam Va Pranasya: By throwing out restraining the breath.

Vishayvati Va Pravrittirutpanna Manasah Sthitinibandhini: Those forms of concentration that bring extraordinary sense-perceptions cause perseverance of the mind.

Vishoka Va Jyotishmati: Or (by the meditation on) the Effulgent Light, which is beyond all sorrows.

Vitragvishyam Va Chittam: Or (by meditating on) the heart that has given up all attachments to sense-objects.

Swapnanidragyanalambanam Va: Or by meditating on the knowledge that comes in sleep.

Yathabhimatdhyanadva: Or by the meditation on anything that appeals to one as good.

Parmanu-Param-Mahatvantosya Vashikar: The Yogi's mind thus meditating, becomes unobstructed from the atomic to the infinite.

Kshinvritterbhijatasyev Manergrihit-Grihan-Hrahyeshu tatsthatdanjnata Samapttih: The Yogi whose Vrittis have thus become powerless(controlled) obtains in the receiver, (the instrument of) receiving, and the received(the Self, the mind and the external objects), concentratedness and sameness, like the crystal (before different coloured objects).

Tatrashabdarthgyanvikalpaiyh Sankirnam Savitarka Samapatti: Sound, meaning, and resulting knowledge, being mixed up, is (called) Samadhi with question.

Smritiparishuddhau Swarupshunyyevarthmatrnirbhasa Nirvitarka: The Samadhi called "without question" (comes) when memory is purified, or devoid of qualities, expressing only the meaning (of the meditated object).

Aitayev Savichara Nirvichara Cha Sukshmavishaya Vyakhyata: By this process, (the concentrations) with discrimination and without discrimination, whose objects are finer, are (also)explained.

Ta ev sabijah samadhih: These concentrations are with seed.

Nirvichar-Vaisharadyedhyatmprasadah: The concentration "without discrimination" being purified, the *chitta* becomes firmly fixed.

Ritambhara Tatra Pragya: The knowledge in that is called "filled with Truth".

Shrutanumanpragyabhyamanyavishaya Visheshарthatvat: The knowledge that is gained from testimony and inference is about common objects. That from the Samadhi just mentioned is of a much higher order, being able to penetrate where inference and testimony cannot go.

Tajjah Sanskaronyasanskarpratibandhi: The resulting impression obstructs all other impressions.

Tasyapi Nirodhe Sarvnirodhannirbijah Samadhi: By the restraint of even, this (impression, which obstructs all other impressions), all being restrained, comes the "seedless" Samadhi.

Bibliography

1. *Asana Pranayama Mudra Bandha* – Swami Satyanand Saraswati
2. *Pranayama – The Art and Science* – H R Nagendra
3. *Yogic Management of Common Diseases* – Dr Swami Karmananda
4. *Yogic Asanas & Pranayama* – Swami Akshaya Atmanand
5. *Yoga for Diabetes* – Dr S S Srikanta, Dr R Nagarathna, Dr H R Nagendra
6. *The Art of Breathing* – R Venugopalan
7. *Restful Sleep* – Deepak Chopra
8. *Techniques of Massage* – S V Govindan
9. *Science of Yoga* –0 Parivrajika Ma Yogashakti
10. *Yoga Simplified for Women* – Smt. Sitadevi Yogendra
11. *Easy Steps to Yoga* – Swami Sivananda
12. *Stretch Your Limbs for balance* – Yoga for long and healthy life – Elise – Browning Miller and Carol Blackman
13. *Facts about Yoga* – Yogendra, Yoga Institute Bombay
14. *Hatha Yoga Simplified* – Yogendra, Yoga Institute, Bombay
15. Yoga for Students : Yogacharya H R Yadav
16. *Sukhi Evam Tandurust Budhape ki ore* – Ramesh Chandra Shukla
17. *Yogasana aur Pranayama* – Ramesh Chandra Shukla
18. *Chakra evam Kundalini* – Ramesh Chandra Shukla

Fit & Fine in BODY & MIND

Hundreds of books are written, every year, on health and fitness, but not many reflect on the connection between the mind, body and spirit. It has been proved beyond doubt that this connection is a vital one and healing of the body cannot take place without the healing of the other two factors. Holistic health is about these three elements. A fitness regime without including all the elements is bound to be ineffective in bringing about 'total health and fitness'.

This book endeavours to unravel the mysteries behind the mind-body connection and shows the path to the ultimate fitness of both, body and mind.

Big Size • Pages: 209

Healing Power of MEDITATION

Meditation is widely accepted as a method to reduce mental tensions and achieve inner peace and tranquillity, leading to spiritual growth. In this book, various techniques are presented in easy step-by-step way starting with simple techniques that can be practised for just a few minutes.

- The power of mantras
- The immense benefits of Pranayama
- Auras and chakra meditation
- The benefits of Kundalini awakening
- Healing through numerous forms of meditation
- Physical, mental and psychosomatic benefits

Demy Size • Pages: 96

Healing Power of Foods

Hippocrates, the father of medicine, recognized that the medical therapy must be consistent with the nature and design of the human body.

He believed that the effective health care could not be separated from nutrition. He strongly recommended prevention of disease through balanced diet with a moderate and sensible lifestyle.

Hippocrates wrote, `Natural forces within us are the true healers of disease... Everything in excess is opposed to nature... To do nothing is sometimes a good remedy.` His philosophy was very much akin to the holistic health perspective of today.

The various foods in this book provide not only nutrition to our body, but prove to be medicinal too.

Demy Size • Pages: 209

Road to Health Care

With ever-rising ground, water and atmospheric pollution, every other day one hears the name of a new disease. Ever since man began drifting away from Nature, he is falling into the trap of a materialistic lifestyle that has desensitised him. Today, we breathe air thick with exhaust fumes, eat processed junk food that has no nutritive value, drink toxic carbonated beverages and lead sedentary lives.

Whatever be your problem – diabetes, blood pressure, asthma, acne, menopause, obesity, stomach ailments, premature ageing or general complaints – this book shows you a safe, natural and enjoyable means to overcome it. Most of the ingredients mentioned in the book are the kind available in home gardens or off the kitchen shelf. Once you have read this book from cover to cover, you need not rush to the doctor every now and then, but will be able to take care of your own and your family's health yourself.

Big Size • Pages: 96

Kitchen Clinic

Home Remedies for Common Ailments

Home remedies and treatment of diseases by domestic plants have been prevalent since the time immemorial in India. The knowledge about the miraculous curing properties of plants is limited to certain people and is passed from one generation to another.

In the present book, the authors describe medicinal uses of 59 plants, which are used in daily life in the kitchen of Indian homes. Botanical names, vernacular names, identification, distribution and medicinal uses of each plant have been given. The book will serve as a guide of home remedies as practiced by our grandmothers, in the middle of night or at odd hours when drug stores are closed. This book gives some alternate ways of controlling earaches, insomnia, minor burns, coughs, eczema, sore throats etc.

Demy Size • Pages: 150

Ayurveda for All

Recent years have seen a tremendous progress in the knowledge and practice of traditional Ayurvedic medicine, not only in India, but the world over.

Once treated with disdain, the exciting discoveries being pioneered by leading research scientists are proving that Ayurveda with its emphasis on health as well as disease is probably the world's most holistic health system.

As allopathic drugs extract a heavy toll in costs and side-effects, more medical many and more people worldwide are turning to complementary medical systems like Ayurveda, Homeopathy, Reiki, Acupressure and many others.

Big Size • Pages: 220

Nature Cure

This book will help understand the methods used by Naturopathy which was given a new definition in India by Dr. Jussawalla several decades ago. You can see why Mahatma Gandhi, Jawaharlal Nehru, Morarji Desai, Meena Kumari and several other well-known personalities resorted to Nature Cure.

The book may help you decide whether you need allopathy for immediate relief or if it is a better bet to change your lifestyle completely and remove the cause of the disease from the root. You will get to know the therapeutic uses of water, sunlight, air, massage, other Naturopathic methods, the right diet, the benefits of fasting, the virtues of vegetarianism, the importance of regular exercise, the value of sleep, the need for fellowship and a mind at peace with itself, the effects of colours, herbs, minerals, vitamins, even the zodiac, the harm from Genetically Modified foods, and so on.

Demy Size • Pages: 208

Yogasanas and Sadhan

Yoga is a great dynamo of power, says the author which one can tap to become a master of oneself and the world.

According to Dr. Satya Pal, the greatest power and energy is within us and 'yoga' alone can help humanity to utilise this physical and mental power to the fullest. Yoga keeps the body and mind sound and hence the author penned this book to show the world, the right way to a healthy body, mind and soul.

The book focuses on:

- The Structure of Human Body
- Yogasanas, Dhyana & Pranayama
- Treatment through Asanas
- Yogic Purification Practices
- Yoga therapy & Yogic Massage
- Yogic Diet and Fasting and many more interesting facts related to yoga and naturopathy.

Demy Size • Pages: 120

A Lifelong Package for Perfect Health

The essential to all natural perfect health insurance

The concept that there is more to health than the absence of disease, that natural approaches enliven our intrinsic healing system, and that the human body is a network of energy and information rather than aggregated anatomical structure has become woven into the very fabric of our modern view of health and sickness, and of life and death.

More than half of healthy, less healthy and sick people of all age and gender regularly access alternative and complementary medical care to keep fit that goes beyond a cut & paste view of human body.

And recognising this ever rising demand of greater choice and access in maintaining wellness in body & mind, this 4-volume set '**Perfect Health**' has been brought out.

Volume 1: Body, Diet & Nutrition

Volume 2: Fitness & Slimming

Volume 3: Health Hazards & Cure

Volume 4: Stress & Alternative Therapies

The result is a total plan, tailor-made for each individual, to reestablish the body's essential balance with nature; to strengthen the mind body connection; and to use the power of holistic healing to transcend the ordinary limitations of disease and aging – in short, for achieving *Perfect Health.*

---

visit us online bookstore: **www. vspublishers.com**